COMING OF AGE
AT THE END OF HISTORY

COMING OF AGE
AT THE END OF HISTORY

Camille de Toledo

Translation by Blake Ferris

Soft Skull Press
Brooklyn

Library of Congress Cataloging-in-Publication Data

Toledo, Camille de, 1976–
  Coming of Age at the End of History / Camille de Toledo.
    p. cm.
  Includes bibliographical references and index.
  ISBN 13: 978-1-59376-197-4 (alk. paper)
  ISBN-10: 1-59376-197-X (alk. paper)

  1. Counterculture. 2. Globalization. 3. Title.

HM647.T64 2008
306'.1—dc22   2007046775

Cover and Interior designed by Luke Gerwe
Printed in the United States of America

Soft Skull Press
An Imprint of Counterpoint LLC
2117 Fourth Street
Suite D
Berkeley, CA 94710

www.softskull.com
www.counterpointpress.com

Distributed by Publishers Group West

10 9 8 7 6 5 4 3 2 1

—How long do we have to go on apologizing for being romantics? Why not stop right now? Here. Boom! All of a sudden. Let us make the desert green with lyrical trees and mocking jays. Let us abandon irony and the fear of naiveté. The cliché is not kitsch. It's merely pretty. So, what do you think?

—You cannot ordain the end of the times of disillusion with a wave of your hand. Cynicism is a strong castle, heavily guarded by powerful armies. You need more than a nice turn of phrase. An insurrection! A hurricane! A noise so insane that it shakes up consciousness. And even then . . . I doubt that this is enough.

"And moreover, that means that to be able to make a diagnosis of one's times, one has to be intoxicated by one's times."[1]

I dedicate this book to Oscar of the Aleph theater, conductor of the *Cabaret de la dernière chance,* Ivry-sur-Seine, to Ghérasim Luca, providential deconstructor of our dead languages, and to all the fish who have leapt out of their bowls to escape boredom.

CONTENTS

THE NEW CAPTIVITY
Which way to the egress?

"If there no longer seems to be any alternative to so-called reality . . . it's not because the real finally stands naked before our eyes. Far from it. What calls itself realism is really a kind of idealism. These days, we live as though underwater, submerged in a representation of the world and of ourselves which forecloses on every objection, every alternative. And this total intolerance is its claim to glory."[2]

"Naturally, it's a coercive technique, but one that the prisoner has to agree to first. Consent must be given from the very beginning; the individual must allow the electronic bracelet to be placed on his wrist. And once the detainee is promised his freedom in return for wearing the bracelet consent is easily acquired."[3]

A man stands still. He's suffocating. Transparent walls rise up around him on all sides, clear as glass, but he doesn't know they are there. There's a ringing in his ears, a vast clamor of voices, opinions, and messages telling him relentlessly that he is free to choose, free to dream, even free to rebel if that's what he chooses to do. It's not the clamor of a department store. It's not talk radio, he's not in a movie theater. Like the six billion other people on the planet, he's locked inside the New Architecture of the United World. He's heard a thing or two about his prison: this world, the world we live in now, is all there is. There's nothing left outside it and there's no other world possible. *Or:* there's no such thing as distance anymore. *Or again:* only capitalism is truly revolutionary. *And finally:* the world today is complete, one and indivisible.

He can't remember where he first heard these ideas. He doesn't know who decided it should be that way. All he really knows is that sometime in the not-so-distant past, capital had licked its lips one last time and swept the last anti-establishment vestiges at the corners of its mouth into its gullet. And boom! the NAUW was here to stay. He'd gone through many changes in his search for a way out. He'd fought to improve the lot of the Third World. Later on, he'd become a Situationist. Next came Trotskyism. Some of his friends from that period are still in prison for terrorism. When punk came along, heroin in tow, he had done both. This, he had figured, might finally be what he had been waiting for. He'd OD, go out with a big fuck *you. Finally, he settled for resignation. And really, resignation wasn't all that bad. After all, the New Architecture of the United World is democratic and generous. In the NAUW human beings are born with equal rights, including the right to happiness. Through education and work every single one of them* has a chance to acquire every single convenience of every modern lifestyle. And finally, doesn't the NAUW guarantee peace among all nations? Doesn't it hold out the promise of economic development to poor countries everywhere?

"Anyway," the suffocating man said to himself, "if capital co-opts everything, even its best and most driven critics, then why fight? You get fed, right? Outrage, resistance, fighting the power, subversion, revolt, revolution—it's all so last century now."

And the suffocating man was not mistaken. Capitalism's project had changed. Capitalism had become so thoroughly modern—so thoroughly postmodern as well—that frankly even those who rejected capitalism looked conservative. From within the corridors of economic and cultural power, now the same power, the malcontents now just looked like people who didn't know how to have a good time. What was their problem anyway? Thanks to the way the New Architecture of the Unified World was laid out, rejecting the establishment was now part of the establishment's very foundation. Abolishing all values had become the only value. You could listen to your poets and your rock stars, you could mix it up, shoot it up, and have your acid visions, it all still ended up being good for the bottom line. The establishment had warmed to its rebels and raging visionaries a long time ago. Now they were sought-after celebrities, picking at caviar with the elite, making copy with their bouts of air rage in first class. In fact, all the aesthetic norms of capital had morphed. The king of pop culture used to be a heavily perspiring white man. No more! Today the old empire has fractured into a thousand provinces, exotic, hybrid, and sensual. World music is the world's music. We've come a long way, baby.

So the suffocating man jumped aboard the NAUW, and surrender was not without some surprises. His name began to appear in print. Journalists and multinational corporations alike smiled on his progress, and behold, their smiles were the same smile.

He discovered that he could turn tricks with his alt-culture savvy. It could make him rich.

No sooner was he on the payroll, he found his salary growing. Rapidly. It was one thing after another. He became an art director with an ad agency, then the publisher of a hip magazine, then a booster for the new economy. Next stop was the host spot on a voyeuristic reality show that fed hungry mainstream audiences showfuls of ever more exotic deviances. And from there, it was a small step to a job with a UN agency created to bring the wonders of modern communication and information technologies to the benighted peoples of underdeveloped countries.

From these experiences our man concluded that humanity's sole destiny was to work toward reform, and reform was only possible under democratic capitalism. It was impossible to go beyond that framework and as for the counterculture, its only possible destiny was the total and specific commodification of every last one of its modes of expression. So why, you might ask, why was this man suffocating? This man, for whom rebellion had proven so lucrative? He had no idea.

He ran his hands along the invisible walls. Back when the barriers were shaggy with coils of razor wire it was all much more simple. When the other side had a name and an address. Beads of sweat oozed from his forehead. A pissed-off looking young guy suddenly rounded a corner and booked past him. They were not all that different from one another, though he figured he had about *thirty years on the newcomer. He watched as the kid pulled two cans of spray paint from his pockets, red and black, and with a flurry of forearms the words* Power is invisible until you provoke it *appeared dripping as if suspended in air along the flank of the invisible barrier.*

The suffocating man tried to keep from smiling, but it was no use—he knew that soon enough the slogan would end up adorning a pair of Nikes. The kid took a step back and watched outraged as his graffiti melted away. Then he reached out and punched the space where a moment ago he had tattooed his anger. His fist sunk deep into the wall. He hit it again, harder, and this time the momentum of his punch carried him right through the wall. On the other side, he found himself confronted by a smiling human resources director who promptly offered him a job at a design studio. "It's 100% employee-owned," human resources enthused, taking the kid by the hand.

As this scene unfolded, the suffocating man absently unbuttoned his shirt collar and groped for the edge of one of the soft walls of the New Architecture of the United World. Fingers grazing the wall for guidance, he took off running, slipped into a small alleyway and began weaving away from the arterials, up the shrinking feeders, farther and farther from the center. After a while he figured he must be reaching the outer edges of the fortifications. Soon, he thought, the walls would be old and crumbling, full of cracks. Instead, he rounded a corner and emerged blinking into what seemed to be some kind of bizarre theme park.

Subcommandante Marcos was digging out scoops of ice cream and whacking them into cones for the visitors, people like, yes, there was El Ché, *pumping away at the joystick of a virtual reality game. They also had this haunted mine ride where you could take an old-timey mine train with a bust of Marx bolted on the front like a figurehead and rocket down into fake caverns.*

My soul has asthma. I mean that the atmosphere of these times causes me severe respiratory distress. It's not the old problems, the familiar problems that we all know by heart. My suffering is less public. None of the usual symptoms here—no coughing fits, no hawking and spitting. I have observed, met, or been a part of almost everything people say exemplifies the spirit of the times, and in every case I have come away from these pathetic excuses for nourishment choking even harder. I need air. That's why I have been rooting through the debris of my 90s for such a long time, looking for a place where I could come up for air, for one or two ideas that could give me some breathing space. I'm sure I'm not the only one. There's no way. I'm willing to bet that the suffocating I'm talking about is a suffocating *we*. The *we* of a generation whose outlook was formed between the poles of two strangely symmetrical dates: 11/9—November 9, 1989—and 9/11, that September day not so many years ago. On one of those days a wall came down, on the other two towers fell. *Boom* behind, *Badaboom* in front. Two times nine, two times eleven, double collapse. Both of those days are history now, but during the years in between, "capitalism" became for me another word for maturity. I mean that I came to understand growing up as the process of resigning yourself to Reality . . . the brute reality of egoism, the idiotic reality of competition, the imbecilic reality of the incentive-driven life and the duty not only to exist, but to exist with a cozy layer of lard on your ass and a protective patty of bullshit on your eyes. Two times nine, two times eleven. Like dust clouds rising from the double collapse, a special kind of consciousness billowed up from the debris of this decade, as yet unaware of itself, mine, ours: 119911. The palindrome-consciousness of my generation. A generation for whom all there was to see in front or behind were immense clouds of dust and debris. But it's worth trying to understand it, this palindrome-consciousness. I don't think anyone really has, not yet anyway. Its elders have gagged it. It's supposed to just shut up. Well, maybe it can make a little noise, maybe it gets to speak a few lines, but only if they're watered-down, sugar-coated, shrink-wrapped, and sanitized for consumption. The plan is to keep its voice stifled until the members of yet another generation grow old, petrified and contaminated, a thousand little renunciations stamped into their faces like crow's-feet. And all this so that when the moment comes for this generation to claim its place in the history books and walk out onto life's big stages, it will be too late. By then, that beautiful spirit forged by the double collapse will have been entirely co-opted, its need for air sated by snack food and other assorted trivialities. This is why I have set out here to document the phenomenon before rot sets in, before life has eaten away what is left of my innocence. I've had it with the sage advice of the compromised and resigned. Let me say right away—I know it's true—our generation—the sons and daughters of the BOOM and the BADABOOM—our generation now has within its grasp the kind of power and the kind of honesty that can work the great changes, that can create real works of art. Every day I watch as our elders shamelessly extend their empire and spread their bullshit around and it makes me nearly blind with rage. Why don't they just finish dying for fuck's sake and take their miserable egos with them, their nostalgia, their State, their sexual liberation, their failed revolutions, their shattered illusions, their political parties, their parliaments and their putrid corpses.

We don't want any more of the history *they* are writing. Here's ours, right here!

For the children of the double collapse, the initial motivation behind the new spirit of revolt isn't economic. It's respiratory. It starts with a vague, unpleasant and overpowering feeling. A stifling feeling of being cornered, boxed in, buried alive! Does that do it justice? It's a violent claustrophobic reaction to the idea that the world is a finished piece of work. That among other things, it has finally been confirmed that there is only one system of political, social, and cultural management available to humanity. You get strangely ill from having your options cut off like this; it's a disease without obvious symptoms. Its first sign is an overpowering sense of powerlessness. Then nausea sets in, it moves up through the gut, chokes the throat and then spreads throughout the entire body. This is the malaise that is driving the spoiled children of the West as they attempt to rediscover the possibility of resistance. Was it just some kind of panic attack? I don't think so. The last twelve years were clogged with despair. If we're still here, it's because we were forced to invent a reason to go on living. We had to forge an outlook that REJECTS RESIGNATION.

"What is a rebel?" Albert Camus asked in 1951. "A man who says no, but whose refusal does not imply a renunciation. He is also a man who says yes, from the moment he makes his first gesture of rebellion. A slave who has taken orders all his life suddenly decides that he cannot obey some new command. What does he mean by saying 'no'?"[4] The market has been systematically co-opting revolt ever since, for 50 years now. The question today isn't any longer *what* does he mean by saying "no." What we need to ask now is why "no" doesn't mean *anything* anymore. Say no to *whom* exactly, to *what*? This *impossibility*, absolute until the demonstrations in Seattle, Prague and Genoa suggested otherwise, is the keystone in our globalized prison's invisible architecture, the linchpin of what I am calling the new captivity. This is the sea into which we were cast as teenagers, where the main choices were limited to despair, suicide or irony. Despair? Despair over a destiny that is finished as soon as it has begun to unfold. Suicide? A way out. Irony? A means of survival. As the walls closed in the wake of the disappointments of earlier generations, principled revolt became increasingly difficult: its causes were discredited, its inspiration was polluted, and its value was restated in terms of the money-making potential of its different poses. This fate was not imposed from above. No one was forced into cynicism. People just heard the same message over and over: "Well, all this has been tried before, and look what good that did." We were already jaded, and anyway, Camus's "no" was beginning to bore us. No one even noticed as the different forms of revolt unraveled, and turned into what were at best quaint sound-bites and at worst marketing strategies. People would express their rage and there would be all this angry noise and every time it all just ended up seeming like a temporary pose. In spite of this, we can still feel the sincerity of that righteous indignation, late at night when we are by ourselves and undistracted by the drone of entertainment. But it has become something obscene, something we must hide from others.

This is how life is in the new captivity. My goal in setting out on this exploratory mission into its invisible architecture has been to try and understand how revolt has been neutralized and how in our resulting helplessness—since there are apparently no other options open—we seem condemned to seek shelter in irony. I want to suggest that our bondage rests on five pillars, five conditions that are the building blocks, as it were, of the impasse our generation finds itself in today. The first pillar has come down squarely in front of History, and so History has stopped moving. The second ensures that anyone attempting to resist will be instantly condemned. The third pillar is the co-option of any and all efforts at subversion. The fourth pillar is a machine that has sucked up everything marginal and spat it out into the mainstream. And the fifth is the dispersion of economic and political power so wide that it has become impossible to confront it. This pentagon has been our school of despair. Between those five walls an entire generation was trained in the sciences of cynical laughter and in the arts of what I am going to call *mass dandyism*.

Sleep Tight

The first pillar of our world's invisible architecture is the *spirit of endings*. It was built as the 80s became the 90s, around the time that people in Moscow were celebrating this new idea—Freedom—with an intensity rarely seen since. I was thirteen years old. The pillar was made out of Berlin stone, stone from the bricks of the GREAT WALL, the same bricks that, now reduced to gravel, were being made into cheap jewelry destined for the flea markets of the West. The stones of Berlin, pocked with bullet marks and scratched by razor wire on the eastern side, colored by layers of counter-culture graffiti on the western side . . . For those who remember those days, these were artifacts of a happy time. A light, pleasant breeze blew through those months. My mother bought me a T-shirt celebrating the date: November 9, 1989. But it only took a few months and several trips through the washing machine for the letters and numbers on the shirt to fade beyond recognition.

The summer before the T-shirt, an article entitled "The End of History?" appeared in the political journal founded by Irving Kristol, *The National Interest.*[5] Prior to that article, the name Francis Fukuyama was known only to a handful of students and academics. The question mark suggested that Fukuyama wanted to avoid jumping to any conclusions, but the damage had been done. The pundits instantly seized on what they recognized as the keystone of the *après*-Cold War's triumphalist rhetoric. The dialectic was over; History had arrived at its final phase, its fulfillment, and would go no further. Now democracy and turbocapitalism walked hand-in-hand like the newly-hitched excreta of a Vegas wedding chapel. The rest of us had no choice but to fall in line with the macabre procession.

Veteran partiers and party-members of the 20th century, connoisseurs of the barbaric delights of that age, I ask you, use your imagination, do you think growing up is easy when your mother is a cemetery? Was Fukuyama right? That's a question for the philosophers, not for me. But take the words "We're at the end of History." Try to listen to that lullaby with the ears of a child. Try to hear how it sounds as the book closes and voices are hushed, as the lights are turned out and the dim figures of the people who put us to sleep slip away with a phrase gentle and disturbing at the same time: *Sleep tight. Sleep tight* was our pillow and our cradle. And we did sleep tight. No missiles kept us awake nights. The crisis was past. We were the happy campers. There was nothing left to do but live happily ever after and sleep tight. We are the children of that funeral elegy. It was plausible enough. It would have been easy to believe that any attempt at creating something is in vain, that writing is just a form of masturbation, that resistance is futile. The various causes that might have given us a reason to keep going were either retro or obsolete, take your pick. Independence? Retro. Alienation? Obsolete. Punk Rock? Retro. Rock and Roll? Obsolete. Unionism? Obsolete. Communism? Retro. Modernity? Outmoded.

Fukuyama caught wind of something that the rest of the world had been smelling for a while. Ever since the mid-80s, there had been something in the air, a hint of something completed, something over.[6] Now the *spirit of endings* was a sold-out show all over the world. Pulling the wings off of the idea of *becoming*, as a child might mutilate a fly, became an international pastime. Preaching that the end times were upon us became sexy. It was sort of a weird thing to get excited about. Apparently, everything was going to vanish, or go extinct, or achieve completion, or whatever . . . But instead of hearing the happy sounds of weddings or baptisms, instead of wedding feasts and champagne, the services we saw being given everywhere were funereal, elegiac. It was the end, and the end was good. These were fat times for obituary writers. At the head of the pack were Hans Belting, a German art historian, and Arthur Danto, an American philosopher a little too obsessed with Warhol's Brillo boxes. "It was a moment—I would say it was the moment—when perfect artistic freedom had become real . . . Everything was permitted, since nothing any longer was historically mandated. I call this the Post-Historical Period of Art, and there is no reason for it ever to come to an end."[7] Snort a few lines from this period, and you get a feeling for it instantly: the name-dropping, the mania for citation, the growing impression of a world mesmerized by its own reflection.

Art had decided that its mission was to join those producing the same dittohead regurgitations of life offered in less tony media. Banality became sacred, and all of the classical aesthetic criteria were henceforth so much gunk caked on the rim of history's dustbin. In the same motion, art denied itself permission to confront society's norms. "If nothing is true," wrote Dostoyevsky in *The Brothers Karamazov*, "then everything is permitted." And if everything is permitted then transgression is obviously no longer possible. That is the contribution the *spirit of endings* has made to our captivity. To celebrate the collapse of a wall they made a urinal into an altar. In the name of liberty, Art and History were relegated to the past and vast swamps of banality were annexed to the present.

This swan song reverberated on through the beginning of the 90s. Not only did it pollute every inch of the reality around us, it stunted our ability to imagine other realities. One very prescient French essayist, Jean-Paul Curnier, put it this way:

> These were the times of decomposition. The sense of completion without any hint of new beginnings that now permeates western democracies is just a figure of the general sentiment writ large. Everywhere, the only important things are endings. The end of utopias, the end of politics, the end of meaning, the end of feminism, of sexual liberation, of full employment, of the golden age, of communism, of History, and topping it all off, the end of modernity itself.

The first edition of *Aggravation* was published in 1996. Curnier had started writing it in the year of Berlin Wall souvenirs and T-shirts. He was ten years older than me, so he had seen each stage of the enormous funeral under whose shadow we were doomed to live. As for our own generation, we were widows and widowers before even getting married. Our future was like a spider web stretched between two chandeliers at a big memorial service. While on the floor below everyone appeared to be weeping, most were actually making barbed remarks under their breath, covering them with more public sniffles and sobs. Well before we had even the slightest ambition to be part of the world, the pallbearers were already carrying the casket of our future towards a common grave. We never did get a look at this future, but we did see the dirty faces of the sextons marching off with their shovels and picks. We never heard the voice of our future, but we did join in the songs of farewell. Hell, we helped to seal the vault. And now the ceremony is over. So go back home! Turn on the TV! Do something! Let old acquaintance be forgot! What humanity really wants is a piece of tinsel and a pretty story. All you really need to worry about is getting busy with your stocks, busy with your cocks, and rocking the rocks in your stupid fucking heads.

We were still playing hopscotch when the writers, political pundits, historians, and critics took up battle stations on either side of the *spirit of endings*. Eventually, it became clear that this was a purely rhetorical war. On one side, the conservatives rejoiced that the end of the world had finally arrived. On the other, the progressives sought salvation through deconstruction. Art was over. Borders and national sovereignty no longer existed. Politics had come to an end. The timing was great, too, because weren't we approaching the millennium? Post-punks, post-rockers, postnationalists, and a lot of other groups with names as silly put their faith in these trendy labels, hoping that they would carry them to a post-world, a world that would still have an after as well as a before. But reality had lost the ability to examine itself through anything more significant than a prefix.[8] The dominant spirit of the present has banished the image of cyclical time, of revolutionary time, and now it only dreams of a future colored in endless shades of gray. Instead of the radically new, all we've got is the cycle of fashion, seasonal novelty. A universe of tiny little variations on the same theme, just with more beats, more bass notes and more nothingness. The novelty item! That's why we keep going back to music stores, to newsstands, to supermarkets, and to bookstores. Post, post, post, after, after, after, new, new, new, neo, neo, neo. The whole bundle of prefixes is repeated with the incantatory passion of a high priestess in heat. Maybe sometimes with good intentions, but IN VAIN! Totally pointless form of behavior here. Even when the larger buildings are obscured by low clouds and fog, the whole game takes place in the framework of democratic capitalism, whatever moves are made at street level. And that's why those of us who had to grow up in the midst of this funeral are so determined to put an end to the spirit of endings.

Farewell Parties

Funerals are often times to rehash old memories, and this one was no different. *He was so this, he was so that, Yes, that night last winter, he looked so happy. Well, what can you do? He's gone now, he went so peacefully . . .* But for us, trying to sit still during the service was a chore. The entire world had chipped in for the enormous white tent raised to welcome the mourners, but we were fidgeting during the drone of the speeches, the uplifting anecdotes, the formal, farewell-party smiles. I would have been out of there in a second had it been up to me. I was thinking of a cute girl I had seen rollerskating in the parking lot outside, brunette, a bit taller than me. But there was no escape from dad's lap, from mom, from grandpa, from the cousins—we were all stuck there, defeated and antsy as the interminable parade of speakers came and went, each one teetering off to the podium far up in front, clutching the microphone with shaky hands and delivering their eulogies.

The most heinous speeches were delivered by the very old, those who had lived through WWII and the 40s. Sometimes they spoke in the name of their dead, other times in the name of those they had killed. Sometimes in the name of their collaboration with the enemy, sometimes in the name of their resistance—however they framed it, the main point was something about defending commerce against all comers. Gentle commerce, the peacemaker, the civilizer. Commerce, the royal road to reconciliation after the brute butchery of the war. Free enterprise: the key to brotherhood! The memorial speeches of the following generation, our parents' generation, were more sorrowful and more resigned. They had dreamt of revolution only to wake up amidst the debris of their shattered illusions. These weren't merely stories trotted out in the intimacy of family gatherings. They were depositions in sensational show trials, testimony delivered collectively, emphatically in endless public investigations launched against both eras—the war years and the 60s—almost before they had even ended. The first of these featured the sinister cortege of the guilty, the Klaus Barbies, the Maurice Papons, then came the obscene hair-splitting over the number of the exterminated, figures that had to be memorized and recited daily, as though people believed this was the only way to stave off, for 24 more hours, the inevitable repetition of the nightmare. The format of the courtroom drama playing on the other channel was a little different. As the sexual revolution got railroaded up front, rival members of the radical left in the studio audience methodically picked each other off. This dismal fare would be interrupted from time to time by commercials brazenly peddling communist nostalgia as accessories for fashionable themes like the entrepreneurial spirit or national security. In each of these shows, humanity's role was reduced to that of a kind of coroner whose duty it was to identify and classify corpses, to figure out who got the monstrous corpses piled up by the Nazis on the one hand, and who got the decomposed corpse of Marx and the carcasses of 1917, 1936, and 1968 on the other. Our elders kept trying to pass them off on one another, batting them back and forth from side to side like millions of gruesome shuttlecocks, blocking the way forward for our generation. As long as this went on, the only choice we were offered was either guilt for the barbarity of WWII or guilt for the naïve faith in revolution.

The first narrative was fashioned after the defeat of the Nazis. Western civilization had just put the finishing touches on its second suicide, in the process inventing a form of political atrocity worthy of the age of mass culture. While some individuals, Primo Levi, for example, devoted their lives to asking how it was possible to go on living in a culture that had so eagerly welcomed the hellish enormity of the war, others just went back to work. For the beast had to be contained at any price. Never again. Never again could this thing be let out. If it were fine-tuned in just the right way, maybe the economy could banish the specter of world war for good.

Enormous expectations, immense hopes were placed in the ability of the economic system to prevent war from breaking out. It just might work—it might be possible to lock up the beast in a cage of free trade.

This was the great hope. Soon afterwards, however, people began to disagree over the nature of the beast. For the economic system designed to end war became an instrument of oppression in its turn. Does anyone still need to be reminded that more than a third of the world's population now lives on less than two dollars a day? The question today is not whether the economy should be more equitable or more just. Everyone wants "justice," whatever they mean by that word. The real mystery is rather why today it has become so hard to criticize the status quo. Why? I'll tell you why. Because we're *still* haunted by the memory of the war. We're terrorized by it. This collective memory was constructed with a stark message: *either you choose free enterprise, or you choose war.* Just look at the 30s: protectionism, nationalism, military buildups, and then horror. It always ends in horror and atrocity. Horror, and then after the horror, the duty to relive the horror every single day in memory. And so always remember, the only way to peace is through open markets and free trade.

The idea that open markets are the only alternative to open war has worked its way into almost every cell and capillary of our daily lives. It streams invisibly through our bodies like a virus, subtly influencing everything we do. Its secret hold on our minds is such that it is hard to believe that any of our thoughts go uncolored by the memory of the war. After all, this is the pretext for the whole deal—today's economic system is literally built on the rubble of WWII. The horror of the past has been distilled into a concentrated liquor. It runs continually from our pores like a nervous sweat, and sweating guilt for the war's unspeakable barbarities, our bodies are engulfed by its reeking vapors.

All throughout the 80s and 90s, war memories buttressed the walls of our prison. I remember the debates over the Maastricht treaty, the endless arguments leading up to the famous referendum that at one point everyone in France thought was going to be answered with a "no" vote.[9] I remember how Mitterand sold the idea of the hyper-common market to the public: it was either this or war. Free trade or the inferno. The only way to say "no" to barbarity was to say "yes" to commerce. Fiscal discipline would keep a reunited Germany in its place and nip any rekindling of its expansionist ambitions in the bud. I remember listening to the grim numerical mantras streaming from the TV news: public deficits would be limited to 3%, national debt to 30%, inflation to 2% . . . With the arrival of the convergence criteria for European economic union, the spirit of endings reached a new nadir of bleakness. Now you could speak truth to power as much as you wanted, you could shout it in the streets, in front of ministry balconies, go tell them that the language of fiscal discipline was the language of death—it didn't keep anyone from falling into line. The convergence criteria were our new straight and narrow, our new creed: don't stray too far from those figures. Be happy in a world without History. Don't make any sudden movements. Remember the lessons of previous generations and for everything else you'll be free to do what you like. Free to be a man or a woman, transgendered or genetic. Free to listen to traditional Neapolitan ditties or Celtic rap. Free! So long as you obey the convergence criteria. This was the message to Europeans. In the media, one tune segued into another—we went from counting days with the French hostages in Lebanon—245, 246, 247, 248 days for Marcel Carton, Marcel Fontaine and Jean-Paul Kaufmann in the 80s, to counting off of the daily deficit figure in the 90s. You could hear sound of an era every night at 8:00. This is helplessness speaking, this is surrender telling you what you need to do, despair teaching you what you need to know. Today's deficit is 3.7%, 3.6%, 3.5%, 3.4% . . . and so on, *ad nauseum*, right up until the coming of the Euro. The memory of the war egging us on, we all raised our voices in unison: Better peace and the common market than the return of the monster.

It is important to listen to this narrative of memory, this story woven of memories and fashioned into a collective memory. It is important to pay careful attention to its comings and goings, its transformations, how it moves from language to language, from mouth to mouth. Sometimes it emerges to quash sudden eruptions of hatred, other times it is told just to trick us. For while it is put to good use when invoked against the extreme right, the same story is also twisted into an instrument used to criminalize the opposition to neoliberalism.

We had only just begun to follow the teachings of one memory when the other captured our attention. This second narrative grew into a funeral march for the 60s. After the disillusion of the 70s, the despair of the 90s was a foregone conclusion. It adopted sarcastic parodies of 60s slogans as its own watchwords, and the radicals, now approaching 50, mustered all their resources in service of submission and cut deals with the establishment reality. The more the spirit of the 60s examined itself, the more disgusted it became and the more arguments for surrender it discovered. "We gave up," it said. "In the end, the revolution just couldn't compete with the attractions of money and power. You won't last long either, you wait," it suggested. "No one resists the global economic system for long."

But there was a consolation for the hippies. Not only were they welcomed back to establishment society, they could rise in it. In Latin America, the heroes of the counterculture still have an aura of innocence, like James Dean or Jim Morrison—by dying early they achieved eternal youth. In Argentina the *hijos*, the orphans of the disappeared, carried on the struggle the Junta had tried to drown with their parents in the muddy waters of the Rio de la Plata. Youthful black and white snapshots of their parents became their icons. Same for Chile and Uruguay. So long as the revolutionaries died young, they could count on returning from the dead. They would remain eternally young. The *hijos* never saw their fathers' bellies grow soft. Their parents had escaped the fate of the aging revolution in the red robes of martyrs; their children would reconstruct their identities on a clean slate. There was no decadent remnant of the past to clear away first.

Meanwhile in Europe, the generation of Jim Morrison was pushing 50. Its members were serenely putting on weight. The hippies had had a chance to preach their sermons and only to then discover that their brand of revolutionary hedonism no longer made good television. The wayward youth of the 90s, the children who ran amok and were shipped off to boarding schools, the 14-year-old party girl who crawled home each morning with the smell of pot on her clothes and dried sperm on her face, they weren't listening. I remember the anniversary well, the 30-year mark, 1968–98. There were special magazine

issues, TV specials, special news reports—all featuring
dinosaurs of the 60s, now become professionals special-
izing in their own bygone youth, recounting the heroic
years of their hormones, ah yes, when one had real blood
in one's veins and real acne on one's face, propelling one
forward to the barricades. Acne forever! Viva hormones!
Before we join that celebration, we should meditate a little on the abyss that separates us from the Ideal, meditate
on all the shattered ideals piled deep in the bottom of
that abyss . . . *Dany le Rouge*[10] is there, now a bloated
sermonizing bore, as repugnant as fat Elvis, desperately
clinging to a chunk of green sod to keep from plummet-
ing farther, to the bottom where the others lie in pieces.
Serge,[11] the former editorialist, now a denizen of talk
shows, the monomaniacal pundit of a republic of couch
potatoes propped up in traction, on the verge of vertebral
collapse. Bernard,[12] the turned-on professor, a somewhat
more encouraging case, suspended over the void. But
what are they still doing there? Any of them? What keeps
them going as they wither away into nothing? When you
run out of inspiration you have to stop pretending that
you still inspire other people. Or else make an exit. Go
off somewhere, somewhere where there's still life, passion and blood, and find a new source of energy. In art,
for example. Or shack up with a younger woman, whatever, but get it from a running spring, not from a stagnant
pond! Look for it in the arena, with the lions . . . Why
waste your time when you've got nothing left to say,
when you no longer believe anything and are interested
only in your own atonement and renunciation? And
what can one say about the other kind of Red Guilt, the
guilt of the Italian Red Brigades, of the Baader-Meinhof
Gang, of the Japanese Red Army? They didn't come out
for unwanted encore after encore, shaking their fat asses

and hogging the spotlight, but they did give the world's protest movements a taste for repentance, they provided the pretext. The bloodstains were too fresh. The violence of the extreme left groups was ineffective. We had to come up with something else. Something beyond the endings, beyond the funeral speeches, beyond what the bloated or the bloodthirsty relics of the 60s had to offer. But what could be done in the tiny space between craven compromise and outright violence?

In the spring of 2001, the journal *Lignes* devoted an entire issue to the "desire for revolution." Two years after the Seattle demonstrations, there were reasons to believe that something was changing. But no. *Niente, nada*, nothing. In his contribution, Jean Baudrillard emptied the idea of content the way one empties a garbage can: "The concepts of desire and revolution defused, neutralized and exterminated one another insofar as they were conflated under the sign of liberation." Jean-Paul Dollé sought to end the debate once and for all: "Today, the question of revolution has been answered. It is impossible, because capitalism has triumphed absolutely, leaving no part of the world untouched by its dominion." Finally, there was Edgar Morin, waxing almost lyrical: "Revolution is a word that I have abandoned. First of all, we have turned it into a myth, because we believed that it held the solution to every fundamental human problem. Afterwards, it was polluted, disfigured, betrayed, and, as Karl Korsch said as early as 1932, it has become simultaneously utopian and reactionary." The candles were extinguished. The wake was drawing to its close. Aging activists very rarely seem to have anything else to do besides indict the errors of their youth. They've spent a third of their lives readying the revolution, then devoted another third to betraying it. The last third they spend explaining the betrayal. One should live in such a way that one dies with no time left to apologize. Nothing is as ugly as that about-face, that apostasy which turns on the desires of the past and confesses them like sins in the hope of being forgiven for desiring. It's not desire's fault. As long as it was only desire, the revolution killed no one. So why beat yourself up about it? There was nothing the matter with the spirit of 1968. The mistake is in apologizing for having been touched by it, as though that alone was enough to make you guilty of every crime committed in the name of revolution—in other times too, in other countries. A terrible mistake that the rest of us, we children of the double collapse, are still paying for today. Now we too must apologize for Lenin, for the massacre of the sailors of Kronstadt, for political police, for the extermination of the Kulaks, for the tartars of Crimea, for the Uighurs, for the victims of the purges, for that other monster, Stalin, for Siberia, for the murderous career of Baader-Meinhof, for the insanity of Shigenobu and the fanatics of the Japanese Red Army.

The moment the revolution itself was put on trial, from the 20th Congress of the Communist Party of the Soviet Union to the opening of the Soviet Archives, from the trial of the Italian Red Brigades to indictment of the sexual revolution, the very idea of resistance became suspect. Such is the atmosphere that we have had to learn to live in.

Together with the collective memory fashioned during the *après-guerre*, the way we have been taught to remember the events of May 1968 has provided a reliable buttress to the established order. The memory of the war gave it a moral foundation by associating free markets with peace. The memory of the 60s protects it by promoting its own disenchantment with revolution.

These two memories worked better than armies. They have won the battle for hearts and minds. "Never forget," they repeated, "that even the slightest gesture of revolt potentially carries within it the seed of mass graves." Stay put. In the name of remembrance, remain calm. Follow the path of the last men. Not the last men of Nietzsche, but the last men of Fukuyama, "men without courage, men made entirely of desire and reason . . ." Forget politics! It's a dirty business filled with dirty people who end up, most of them anyway, covered in dirt themselves before the history books catch up with them. Instead, spend your free time contemplating the horrors engendered by the passions of your fathers, spend it contemplating their failures. If you really want to take part in the world so badly, if buying a TV set is just not going to do it for you, then at least work to defend the established order and help it protect us from the past. That's what's on the menu here.

In school, I learned that there were two ages of power in the modern era: the power by divine right, which was the foundation of the European monarchies, and power derived from natural law, which placed sovereignty solely in the hands of the people. The French Revolution marks the historical junction between these two regimes, with the beheading of Louis XVI symbolically marking the death of the old order. The third age of power was created out of the ashes of World War II. This time, the roots of power were neither divine nor in the people. This time, power's legitimacy is founded wholly on memory—the total memory of total horror. Its principle goes: The world economic order is legitimate since, through free trade, it guarantees peace. Dissidence needs to be repressed since it can potentially develop into isolationism, nationalism, and then barbarism. It follows that it hardly matters if the people are for or against the first principle since in any case it is the economic order that keeps the peace, not the people. Democratic legitimacy decapitated the king; now mnemonic legitimacy has decapitated the people.

We have left the democratic era behind. One day we'll have to face it. For it was only a phase, one of the better ones, to be sure, but now the time has come to turn the page. Until they can bid farewell to democracy, today's dissident forces will be unable to tear themselves from the grave of the nation-state they cling to like a forlorn Sicilian widow. Let's finish our grieving and get back on track. It's better to attack the principle of power, not its alibi: let us leave democracy right there where mnemonic legitimacy has left it—in the abyss, in pieces, along with the other corpses. "There are no duties of remembrance," says the Jean-Luc Godard film *Éloge de l'amour*, "only a right to forgetfulness." This line spoke to me when I first heard it because it offered me a way out, a path that led out of the captivity. Because the obligation to remember has transformed itself into a repressive force, revolt ought to begin with forgetting. André Gide wrote in the opening pages of *The Immoralist*: "I do not want to remember, I believe it would hamper the future and damage the past." This also spoke to me. It helped me dispense with the obligation my aging predecessors had invented to keep discontent in check. But our memory, alas, has become so consolidated, so institutionalized that it is off-limits to questions it. Take a second to think of the storm of insults and criticism that await any man or woman bold enough to stand up openly for their right to forget. They'd be humiliated, they'd be put in the stocks with the revisionist historians and similar creatures and falsely accused of wanting to deny the very existence of the monster. Jean-Luc Godard dared to go there, at the risk of being understood by no one, and sure enough, no one understood him. When the collective memory is bent to serve an unjust order, then the right to forget it becomes a legitimate act of resistance.

Situationism Normal All Fucked Up

The third pillar of the new captivity came to us disguised as a means of resistance: the critique of the spectacle. I wasn't any less gullible than the rest of them. Gullible, I say, because after the failure of revolutions near and far, the renunciation of the radical left and the ruse of memory, with the Situationists I thought, I hoped, I had come across the sole remaining subversive strategy. Nope. Some months had passed since the fall of the Berlin Wall. Market democracy had consolidated its total monopoly on destiny. With the help of travel agencies, the rest of the world had dwindled into little more than a collection of exotic tourist destinations. The spectacle went on about its business, replacing the world with itself. "You can't touch anything anymore," an enlightened homeless person would remind me each morning I passed him on the way to school. During this period I had been searching with all the fire of my adolescence for ideas that could point the way to a different world, a window carelessly left ajar, a place where I could stop and breathe some fresh air. By chance, I walked into a bookstore on rue Gît-le-Cœur in Paris. The shop had pleasantly outdated name: *Un regard moderne,*[13] a modern outlook. Sandwiched between kebab shops and clothes boutiques, it was barely visible. Inside, it was so full of books that you could barely move around. On one side, American comics, manga, and photo books rose to the ceiling, on the other, shelves were crowded with seditious political tracts and anthologies of dissidence, and in the middle was a heaping pile of unidentified literary objects. There was a refreshing atmosphere of old-fashioned censorship and the consequent naughtiness in the air—to enjoy the pleasures of liberation, you have to invent imaginary taboos. Here *Un Regard Moderne* had succeeded admirably. In this shop, anarchist pornographers cohabited with opium-smoking revolutionaries and Isidor Isou[14] ate his naked lunch while Johnny Rotten spat in André Breton's face. In a corner, Artaud trembled as incandescent lesbians licked his organs, a spectacle watched by heretical monks and filmed by a belching Pier Pasolini. Greil Marcus's *Lipstick Traces* had not yet come out in French, but the web of references he sketched in that book was already stretched across the loaded shelves of that shop. It was dark by the time I got out of the bookstore. It was cold outside. The names I had noted down seemed to me to have an almost magical ring to them, and Guy Debord's was at the top of the list. But it wasn't long before his ideas lost their bite for me and the magic evaporated. Like the stones of the Berlin Wall, the exploits and ideas of Situationism would soon dwindle into fashion accessories.

With each new Situationist tract I digested, the movement seemed more and more tame to me. But the Situationists were suddenly in vogue again. The *habitués* of trendy art openings and street demonstrations alike came to feed at the Situationist trough. Journalists culled its texts for material to spice up their TV shows. Artists mined their work in search of new ways to shock. American media activists used their ideas to subvert the reigning commercial icons.[15] Almost imperceptibly, advertising strategists and CEOs appropriated bits of Situationism to spice up their image. Eventually,

Situationism established itself as one of the ideological references of Internet culture. With a little Situationism, you could go from being a protester to being a performer, move from art to art criticism, then into advertising and television. You could begin with underground music and wind up in international marketing, go from counterculture to consultant. As this happened, its critical potential leeched away and Situationism itself was transformed into intellectual capital for the production of the spectacle. It became a little toolkit for the audiovisual citizen and a practical guide to fashionable subversion. Reading the last lines of the preface added to the 1992 pocket edition of *The Society of the Spectacle*, I could only smile:

> This book must be read with the knowledge that it
> was intentionally written to harm spectacular society.

Before my eyes, I watched as Debord's combat was transformed into another amusement park for the overeducated. The democratization of Situationism had created a new situation. The critique of the spectacle had become a spectacle itself, exemplified by the reality show, and irony and subversion were norms—one of the subsidiaries of the production company Endemol, creators of the hugely popular French reality show "Loft Story" is called "*La Société du spectacle.*" Subversion was no longer at the service of the forces of revolt and resistance, now it was just one more skill that interested human resources departments. Sure, artists could give it another name, they could declare it obsolete, they could choose another, more academic term like *decontextualization*. Counterculture people seeking an alternative label for their media actions might call it *culture jamming* instead—where you monkey with an advertising message in one way or another to turn its intended meaning on its head. The creative staff at ad agencies had recourse to the concept of *disruption*,[16] while journalists could busy themselves with "offbeat" content. In every case it's just good old Situationist subversion adapted to the needs of a specific group of end-users. The arguments over the definition of a work of art, of commerce, of the production of the spectacle and of how these enterprises might or might not be hostile to one another fused into ONE final subversion of the subversion of the subversion of the subversion of the subversion of the subversion of the subversion of the subversion.

For many years, Situationist writings enjoyed an almost clandestine status. You found them in the back of the shop. The print runs were low, the books scarce. One never made reference to the gang of drinking buddies that made up the Situationist International without a certain paranoia. "Circumstances have lent almost everything I've done a certain air of intrigue," Guy Debord wrote in the first volume of *Panegyric*. In the *Nouvel Observateur* of May 22, 1972, journalists were already writing about him as though he was part of a vast left-wing conspiracy: "The author of *The Society of the Spectacle* has always appeared as the discreet but indisputable ringleader . . . at the center of the shifting constellation of brilliant subversive conspirators of the Situationist International, a kind of icy chess master, rigorously carrying out moves that he has planned out in each detail." In the United States, in England, in Italy, in Holland, and even in France, the conspirators' texts were read only by small circles of initiates. Sure, a *mode situ* had swept through the spring of 1968 in France, and media provocation enjoyed a brief fad at the port of Amsterdam . . . But there was plenty of time to forget Situationism after that. After the beginning of the 70s, Debord chose to go silent. Out of elitism, to avoid selling out—to go off and drink, more than anything else. Twenty years passed, during which time his only public appearances were accidental sightings in nondescript bars.

Only for a few years between the release of *Commentaries on the Society of the Spectacle*, in 1988, and the late afternoon of November 30, 1994, when Debord placed a rifle barrel against his heart and pulled the trigger, did his ideas win broader recognition. In 1989, a major retrospective entitled "On the Journey of a Few People Across a Fairly Small Period of Time: The Situationist International, 1957–1972" traveled from the Centre Pompidou in Paris to the Institute of Contemporary Art in London. On October 20 of the same year, the book review section of *Le Monde* ran an article entitled "Know an Individual Named Debord?" Phillipe Sollers, a critic more known for his bemused preciosity than for his militant activities, had finally discovered Debord and he proceeded to load the front page of the literary supplement with a long praise piece, as if apologizing for the fact that the author had been under his radar for so long:

> I'd like to go ahead and talk about a book that no one will talk about, or hardly. A book as destructive and as invisible in broad daylight as Poe's *Purloined Letter*. A book that tells the truth that no one wants to hear, a pin jabbed into the overinflated balloons of commerce . . . The clandestine activities of Guy Debord could fill many pages, this French writer whose name a few initiates will recognize; he is by far the most original and most radical thinker of our time.

Radical? With this blessing, whatever claim to being a radical Debord might have had went up in smoke. Subversive? Henceforth only to himself.[17]

The Zeitgeist needed a Debord. Since everything now was ONE, contained, englobed in the same system and facing the same future, thought needed to hold on to a semblance of dissent, for without dissent it would die. The critique of the spectacle was its life preserver. Without it, there was the risk that the world would lose itself in its own reflection. Centuries of dialogues, debates and struggles would be swept away by the force of this great sophism: only two modes of political management exist: communism and capitalism. Communism is dead. Ergo, capitalism is the only mode of political, economic, and social management. The writings of Debord made a perfect shelter, a cozy room from which one could criticize the world while smoking Toscani cigars. "Today," (Sollers again, this time in the communist daily *L'Humanité* in 1992) "with the black hole left by the collapse of the Soviet empire, I'd like to know where else besides in Debord one can find the concepts needed to understand the new unreality that's now being held up to us as the only reality."

So one clung to Situationism quite sincerely, for it taught the art of survival in face of the great eclipse of reason. And then very soon after, distress gave way to pleasure: one no longer challenged the real, but its image. Way more fun. One no longer railed against injustice, but against the spectacle's exploitation of injustice. Way more sexy. One no longer resisted commerce, but battled the simulacra of commerce. Way more cool. Social criticism merged with film criticism to become a generalized critique of representation. Since reality was a given, only the frame could vary. And the frame is chic, sophisticated.

All of a sudden, the critiques founded on the real became vulgar and tiresome. The seduction of the image was too strong. With Debord, we were all potentially directors, cinematographers, semiologists, artists, dissidents, jaded and mocking documentarians of our own existences. The SI, the cinema, and subversion became one . . . how perfect! And intelligence decided that it was saved because it had deconstructed its own gaze. It didn't realize that in doing so it was devouring its own eyes.

The critique of the spectacle took the spirit of revolt and transformed it into a kind of mass-market dandyism. The times were ripe for an indifferent, even apathetic attitude to flourish. By shifting the issue from reality to its representations, the critique of the spectacle made it possible to adopt such an attitude. Rather than being a militant dandyism operating outside society's norms, an elite pursuit that freely traced diagonal paths through the squared-off fields of other peoples lives, the new form of revolt was a sort of shared indifference accessible to all, a *dandyism of the masses*. The hyperindividualism bred by the belief that everything was spectacular and that the spectacle was everything ended up creating a world of prefabricated non-conformity, a community of snide smugness where one made provocative remarks that sounded subversive on the surface, but were merely jaded. I belonged to that world. Oscar Wilde got sent to prison. British society isolated him and by condemning him gave meaning to his excesses. That's what I call militant dandyism. On the other hand, the dandyism of the 90s was only tenuously connected to revolt, via the network of references that linked the critique of the spectacle, subversive practices, the search for the offbeat, and the dis-instantiation of the real. I'm speaking from experience, because I myself made the journey from revolt to mass dandyism, and all I got out of it was access to an overtolerant club of people in love with their own sophistication, a bunch of jaded, vaguely suspect characters. The steps of that journey are easy to recall: in the beginning . . . the spirit of revolt such as Camus defined it so simply: a man who receives one order too many and says *no*. Then came Fukuyama and the memories constructed by the preceding generations, which taught the renunciation of idealism. From out of the past comes Guy Debord, with him you could at least negotiate your survival. This is how revolt goes into its visual, aesthetic period. As it replaces the critique of the existent with a critique of the image, a shift occurs. The real is only taken into account as art, insurrection appears only through aesthetics, revolt only as a pose, and injustice only as spectacle. Those who grew up with something like passion in their blood then adopt an inconsequential dandyism where the pose is everything and revolt is no longer anything.

Debord saw that things would end up this way, probably out of lucidity, maybe out of despair. You have to read him a second time to see this in his work, you have to listen to his prose as though it were a mirror to see this vicious circle, closed in on itself definitively, where thesis after thesis just seals the closed circuit running between man and capital that much more hermetically. This is no longer theory, it's like the repetitive music of the minimalists. Thesis 42: "The spectacle is the moment when the commodity has attained the *total occupation* of social life." Should you take refuge far from the great cities, you will be quickly discouraged. Thesis 57: "The society which carries the spectacle does not dominate the underdeveloped regions by its economic hegemony alone. It dominates them *as the society of the spectacle.*"

Situationism is not a system of critical thought, but rather a how-to for compromise. It was on page 35 of *Panégyrique* that I found the key. Debord writes:

> In a fit of anger, a queen of France once reminded the most seditious of her subjects: 'Imagining that one is capable of revolt is already revolt' . . . The mind goes round and round in circles and returns to itself after long, eccentric orbits. Every revolution becomes part of history, yet there are no revolutions in history; the rivers issuing from revolutions return to where they began, to flow once more.

1988, 89, 90, 91, 92, 93, 94 . . . The years of our adolescence. The time in which the unfinished sonnet of Margaret Thatcher, "there is no alternative," was completed by the angry words of a queen. In citing his queen, Debord signed a tragic armistice: even the critic of the spectacle acknowledged his defeat. Revolt had lost the battle of the real. The front that it had opened on the battlefield of the image had collapsed. A hope, a tactic and a battle objective vanished in one fell swoop.

I only recently understood how Debord dovetailed with Fukuyama, how together they laid the foundations of the new captivity. It is not at all easy to put them in the same bag: one was an alcoholic hermit and the other helped define American foreign policy during the Reagan years. Nevertheless, different as they are, the consequences of their thought are identical. Each of them described the same destiny, one in which the dialectic of History was dead, co-opted or useless, contributing at the same time to our despair and our abdication. Moreover, Debord came first: as early as 1988, or a year before the publication of Fukuyama's article on

"The End of History," he announces the final absorption in *Commentaries on the Society of the Spectacle*. He writes: "The earlier worldwide division of spectacular labor between the rival reigns of concentrated spectacularity [democratic centralism] and diffuse spectacularity [liberal democracy] has given way to their fusion in a single form of integrated spectacularity." The vocabulary is somewhat more tortuous than Fukuyama's but Debord cared little about being understood. Being right was good enough.

So what about us? What will become of us? Suicide? Or will we go in search of an elsewhere you can get to without dying? Will we decide one day to unfurl our revolt and our indignation so that they can be sucked up onto the stages of the spectacle? Probably. Not a big deal. There's some good in makeup anyway. It makes you better looking. Whether the decision is made on purpose or through coercion, it must be made. Better to do it on purpose. That way you can grow old without growing bitter. That way you become someone that people like to hang out with. You have some fun. You PLAY THE GAME. And there are other arguments for dropping your scruples. Like the one that goes "You have to be on the plane to hijack it." After September 11 you didn't hear it put quite that way. Nowadays one just comes right out and admits to being a parasite. You *choose* to be one. Eating away at the system, you see? With the dialectic, there was an exterior, a beyond. The spectacle turned it into a polished, well-policed interior. See you later dialectic! *Au revoir*! There's no option left but infiltration, becoming a parasite of the system. Such are the conditions under which revolt can occur in the age of the new captivity. We're living in the belly of the beast now. You attach yourself to the gut or the colon and suck away until the beast gets sick. Only the beast almost never gets sick. The beast is tough. But it's no big deal, for the more you root around inside, the higher you get promoted. On the other hand, the beast does not tolerate sleeper cells, malcontents or those who are beyond redemption. Occasionally, they manage to shake things up, even frighten it a bit, but it never goes any farther than that.

Cringe

The fourth pillar of the new captivity orchestrated the disappearance of power in its two traditional forms: political and economic. From that point forward, the representatives of political and economic power have been . . . well, they've been on a sort of business trip, a trip that's probably an alibi for some adulterous liaison, and they vanished completely from radar. They became nomadic, untouchable. We no longer knew to whom we were to address our complaints. Power drifted subtly back and forth through networks of international treaties, multinational corporations, and financial markets. "I'm totally ready to throw Molotov cocktails," you said to yourself after class, "but at whom?" "Should I throw them at California retirees, or at the punk who traded in his Doc Martens for a stockbroker's suit?" Power was no longer visible except under the guise of these ridiculous icons. Its headquarters had been transformed into a bank of facades with nothing behind them—Nike, for example, now subcontracts the lion's share of its production work so that the company proper can focus on the intangible, on its brand image. To fully appreciate this vanishing act all you needed to do was to stop for a moment and remember the way the world looked before it happened. Every once in a while there were still taboos, still instances of censorship. It didn't really matter exactly what they were so long as there were still a few walls to tear down. In the 60s in the famous photos Gilles Caron took around the Sorbonne in May 1968, the confrontation was one of flesh and bone. The demonstrators' target was a superstructure made of ideology and concrete. These days, however, you have the G8 representatives hiding out on a boat off the coast of Genoa to avoid contact with the crowds. The WTO deported itself to out-of-the-way Qatar to keep the people at bay. The organizers have floated the idea of holding future summits in cyberspace. Thus, once mature, the new captivity became a universe of two-way mirrors in which power enjoyed the attributes of gods; it became intangible, transcendent, and omnipresent.[18]

All throughout my adolescence, I watched the crowned heads of the world join in a collective cringe. I watched them bow down one by one in infinite reverence. It reminded me of those Russian dolls where each figurine opens to reveal another, smaller one that in turn conceals another, even smaller, and so on to infinity . . . Such was the fate of anyone who tried to trace responsibility for the damage wrought by the system. Lift up one mask and there was another, never a face. You could keep pulling off the masks until there was nothing left but a gaping hole, and from that void oozed the despair of the early 90s. Ask who was responsible and you risked falling in yourself. If a worker was laid off, if a peasant was thrown off his land, if a region was polluted, if a culture was destroyed, the anger generated was simply sucked into that abyss, along with any potential for revolt. Nothing remained but a chain of individual wills amplified by networks of machines. I saw this clearly when I interviewed the president of the world's most powerful pension fund, CalPERS, an institution whose mission is to finance the retirement of California's civil servants by investing their savings. Bill Crist was a guy with a handsome mustache and lots of good intentions. A former economics professor, he spoke of his fund as though it were a charity organization. "I have a million small investors, civil servants like her, for example," he said, pointing to his humbly-dressed assistant, "who are counting on me for their retirement. I used to be a civil rights activist and a union organizer . . . but it became clear to me that it is useless to fight from the outside. You have to fight capitalism from the inside." From the inside! One more time, I heard those magic words of abdication, bringing the old nausea back with them. Everything was *inside*, nothing was left outside. And it wasn't me saying it, it was a former civil rights activist and union leader, a man now in charge of more than a billion dollars, who represented more than a million civil servants . . . As we were sitting there in his office, he asked me what I wanted to do. I wondered whether it was possible to visit the trading room. We walked down the long corridor and Bill Crist opened a door. There it was! Computers, price curves. A Bloomberg TV feed flickered from monitors suspended in the corners of the room. Traders vibrated with activity, buying and selling. At the time, I had been working on a fable called "A Day in the Life of a Tire," one of those exercises where you follow the life of some product from raw material to end-use and then try to derive a moral from the story. I had begun my journey in the hevea plantations of southern Thailand, where natural rubber is harvested. The small growers had come to the conclusion that the Chinese middlemen who bought their harvest were to blame for their poverty, while the buyers explained to me that their hands were tied by the multinationals that set the rubber prices. The Thai Minister of Agriculture himself told me as much. There was nothing he could do. So I went to Akron, Ohio, to the headquarters of Goodyear to talk to *their* president, a nice Egyptian guy named Sam Gibara. During our talk, he kept on repeating how it was the "market" that was responsible. "And among the most important actors in that market," he told me, "are pension funds." And that's how I wound up at CalPERS talking to Bill Crist, in that room where the money belonged to Mr. Everyman, that is to say, to no one. Power no longer appeared under the sign of the pyramid. Now it had become a chain of hourglasses open at the top and bottom to a swarm of minute actors: tiny workers of the land on one side, and small investors on the other. Only the level of unhappiness changed. For the retirees of California, it was an unhappiness with life-support, a small home in a Bay Area suburb and a choice of baseball and football on the TV. For the Thai growers, it was the rawest poverty, devoid of assistance besides the meager aid they might receive from the local cooperative, 1,000 trees to bleed each day, a few microcredits and a barking dog in the street in front of a ramshackle hovel. An unhappiness vulnerable to bad weather. Between these two extremes, there was business, cabling, the information superhighways and its nodes of control, dispersed power, a family fortune here, an inheritance there, themselves only bottlenecks where wealth builds up before flowing out elsewhere. So whose fault is it? Football's? The barking dog's? Is bad weather to blame? Is Thailand? Is San Francisco?[19]

To better understand how this vanishing was accomplished, I reopened the old and dog-eared books of that sage skinhead, the great master of rebel bodies and deviants, of the sick, the queers and lesbians, the one to whom I owe much of my own carnal curiosity: Michel Foucault. Incidentally, I have to admit that I tried for a long time to find a pair of glasses just like his. Those glasses seemed to sum up the period perfectly—thick and black on the top of the rims, like ersatz communist intellectuals used to wear, and delicately circled on the bottom, as if to suggest a world snapped up by structure. Alas, they didn't make them anymore. Not trendy enough for opticians, not valuable enough for antique dealers, not funky enough to be included among the *situ* bling-blings and T-shirts in the artier flea markets. When I began to reread Foucault he seemed outdated as well. He had taught me about the first dematerialization of power, when power shifted to intermediary institutions to irradiate bodies and souls. He showed me that the state itself could no longer be the target of revolt; only the current flowing from power was accessible to criticism. He wrote of the myriad conditions imposed on the flesh, of the secondary sites onto which discipline applied its power. The battlefield had been extended to the peripheries of the state apparatus, and so education, psychiatry, and the military came under the scrutiny of the critic. Yet in terms of liberation, there was only feeble progress. From now on, criticism was to turn its gaze elsewhere, above our heads, towards the shifting non-space where power now drafted its orders in utter secrecy.

In *Discipline & Punish*, Foucault suggested that an examination of the development of carceral techniques would reveal the way modern power operated. He sifted through the past, studying implements of torture, the remarks of executioners, the sentences of kings, and the darker passages of judiciary gazettes. From these journeys through the Archive he returned with a masterful, brilliant, remarkable symbol that would become *the* metaphor for power for years to come: the Panopticon. "A circular building wrapped around a central tower with large windows looking out on the interior façade of the circle. The peripheral building is divided into cells running its entire width. They have two windows, the first facing the outside and allowing light to flood the entirety of the cell. It then suffices to station a single watchman in the central tower and fill each cell with a mental or medical patient, a criminal, a worker or a student."[20] I was a quick study and, emulating my master, set out somewhat more modestly to sift through the present. I checked out the French National Assembly's 1997 report on prisons, and in this book I found a rather pathetic and burlesque counterpart to the form Foucault had chosen to embody modern power: the electronic bracelet, a new type of control that was being proposed as an alternative to incarceration. Even the name was ridiculous. I mean, *electronic bracelet*? The way it tied fashion to surveillance, jewelry to control . . . it reminded you of a marketing gimmick from a tacky online store. I even fantasized about buying one to show off at the beach. The Assembly heard the presentation of one Eric Lallement, "Undersecretary of Organization and Operations, Field Staff, Department of Corrections." He took care to explain that the technique was already in use in Holland, Canada, the U.S., and the U.K. This is how he described the system:

> It is a plastic bracelet with a fiber optic cord running through it. Cutting the bracelet automatically triggers an alarm. The bracelet contains a device that emits a continuous signal, and is approximately three times thicker than a watch . . . It is not particularly pretty . . . The second technical element is a device that

is installed at the residence of the person or the place where the person is to be surveiled . . .

This device is connected to a telephone link and generates an alarm if the person moves out of a radius of 50 meters from the device. It emits a signal regularly, about once every minute approximately, to which the bracelet responds. When there is no response because the person has moved out of a 50 meter radius, an alarm is generated and then we go to the next technical element, which is the place where alarm will be received . . . Finally, the last technical element is the surveillance center where all the information is compiled . . . This place can be inside a penal establishment, inside a halfway house, at a probation site or in any other place deemed appropriate.[21]

Two of the principles Foucault saw embodied by the Panopticon also apply to the electronic monitoring bracelet. First, the asymmetrical relationship that allows the watcher see the watched without being seen. Second, the internalization of the mechanism of control by the prisoner, making him "the principle of his own subjection." "The individual subjected to a field of visibility, and who is aware of it, himself becomes the agent of the constraints placed upon him by power—he spontaneously applies them to his own person." On the other hand, the monitoring bracelet explodes the site of the power relation: no more prison cell, no more circular building, no more center, no more periphery—just a broadcast antenna, a receiving antenna and nomadic poles of surveillance. All that is needed is to enlarge the free-roam zone. Within these limits, we can come and go as we please, desire, amuse ourselves, rebel. We have the right to create, to imagine, to dream freely. We are not under any constraint at all, since as we move, the signal of the bracelet moves with us, seeming to expand the range of our liberty. In the same way, power's new intangibility creates a form of incarceration without walls. All you have to do is look at the financial press. IN RESPONSE TO POOR MANAGEMENT IN ARGENTINA, SANCTIONS HAVE BEEN APPLIED . . . As soon as a country steps out of the magic circle, alarms begin to go off in the remote centers of power. AFTER YEARS OF IGNORING ITS BALLOONING DEBT, FOREIGN INVESTORS ARE SENDING A SIGNAL TO MEXICO TO GET BACK ON TRACK. Financial markets send signals. They beep. They launch volleys that sometimes are harmless and other times mortal. They supervise. Day after day, market indicators are so obsessively scrutinized—national debt, deficits, gross national product and other, even grosser, things—that in a fate similar to that of the prisoners of the bracelet, the liberty of entire peoples is magnificently annihilated in favor of an *appearance* of liberty, an *authorized range*.

A Dried Locust

The fifth pillar of the new captivity is almost too familiar to my generation to even mention here. I'm talking about *co-option*. The very word speaks volumes to those who like me, ran to the counterculture for shelter. For this reason, I won't go into its history. I'll leave it to each reader to stew in his or her own memories: rock & roll, Malcolm McClaren, rap, the hollow cheeks of junkies popping up in the spreads of glossy fashion magazines . . . whatever it is. By absorbing the margins, capitalism has managed to get the avant-garde, the underground, and marketing seminars singing the same tune. It took decades for white rock to finish looting the heritage of American blacks but things move much faster now. Today, culture is created, understood and accepted as a commercial product from the very start. As anarchist Hakim Bey points out in *Immediatism*, "It has been noticed that all the more advanced and intense art-experiences have become recuperable almost instantly by the media, and are thus rendered into trash like all other trash in the ghostly world of commodities . . . Everything delicate and beautiful, from Surrealism to Breakdancing, ends up as fodder for McDeath's ads; 15 minutes later, all the magic has been sucked out, and the art itself dead as a dried locust. The media-wizards, who are nothing if not postmodernists, have even begun to feed on the vitality of 'Trash,' like vultures regurgitating and reconsuming the same carrion, in an obscene ecstasy of self-referentiality. Which way to the Egress?"[22]

During the 90s, this festival of vultures was completed by two big events which allowed capitalism to fully co-opt the spirit of revolt and integrate it into the heart of consumer society. By superimposing the rhetoric of the "new economy" over the communist utopia of a classless society and by touting diversity as an aesthetic norm, it was able to impose what some friends of mine and I have called the "Economics of Permanent Revolution," what with a bit more marketing savvy, you might refer to as "Rebellionomics," the economics of the rebel age. You could even stretch it into a business book: *Protest for Profit*. But it was getting late, and anyway, we weren't marketing consultants, so we left it there, sticking with those three words that seemed to explain our predicament. "The Economics of Permanent Revolution" describes a system of capital accumulation based on rebellion and protest. From this modest insight, we drew an even more shocking conclusion: capitalism is now and for all time the only authentically revolutionary system. Anyone who denies it is a reactionary.

It was in the U.S., around 1992 or 1993, that capitalism's aesthetic norm shifted. I learned this from Naomi Klein's book *No Logo*. During her college years, Klein was immersed in identity politics. She was furious that so few women, African-Americans, Puerto Ricans, Asians, gays, and lesbians were present in the canon. "A great number of our battles dealt with questions of 'representation', a rather vague rubric of grievances directed primarily at the media, university curricula and the English language."[23] I could imagine this blessed moment in the history of the American conscience, where revolt was limited to defending quotas, I could see young Naomi and a few earnest teenagers wringing their hands together on green campus quads. It was a perfectly defined struggle, with no gray areas. More African-Americans, more women, more Puerto Ricans . . . this ethnic opportunism directed its criticism less at power itself than at the conditions of holding power. Identity politics served the same purpose for American anger that the critique of the spectacle had for European internationalism: it was a refuge for dissidence. At least until something better came along . . .

As she moved through college, Naomi watched as the good cause fell apart. Before she had even begun her long inquiry into the strategies corporations used to seduce young people, she witnessed her own co-option, women, African-Americans, Puerto Ricans, queers, dwarves, whatever, all of her precious minorities were transformed before her eyes into fodder for advertising messages. A junkie with a needle in one arm and a bottle of Pepsi in the other was the pinnacle of hip. "The brands seemed to

47

say to us, you wanted diversity, here you go."[24] One after another, the identity groups' demands for representation were met by commerce, and doubts began to creep into her well-intentioned heart. "The crowning of sexual and racial diversity as pop culture and advertising's new superstar clearly created a kind of identity crisis."[25] Elbowing art aside, capitalism took over the business of critiquing its own aesthetic. Diversity replaced white conformity, and business widened the spectrum of its own discourse to englobe everything that the counterculture had formerly represented: the bizarre, the eccentric, the mixture of belief systems. All these became the latest thing in makeup for capital. And as it was brushed onto the pages of glossy magazines, the fellow-travelers of dissidence were left to leaf through their memories. The avant-garde was no longer avant anything. Everything that had once been relegated to the margins of culture now awoke to find itself at the epicenter.

While on the surface, some observers were right to worry that: "in the nice neighborhoods of the world's largest cities, the spice of diversity is giving way before an explosive offensive of standardization, homogenization and uniformization,"[26] the blossoming reality was completely different. To uniformity, brands preferred the image of an adorable exoticism. It became less interesting to sell a monoculture than to "supply each individual, across the entire world, with a kind of spice mix. At the end of the 20th century, the marketing spiel was coming from the mouth of Ricky Martin, not the Marlboro Man: a bilingual mixture of North and South, of Latino and rhythm & blues, all of it wrapped up in the sing along lyrics of an international party."[27] This was sadly confirmed for me when I met with the communications director of McDonald's France. "Our clocks are set to local time," he explained. Touting the company's global reach was too ostentatious, too egocentric. He corrected himself: "*Chez McDo*"—he started every sentence this way—"we've set out to adapt our production to the diversity of cultures, to the environment." And while he droned on about the virtues of the latest French-style McDonald's combo, I recalled an article by Jean-Marie Messier, the now-fallen super-CEO of Vivendi. A few weeks earlier, he had published a kind of hymn to diversity in the pages of *Le Monde*. He had his top advisers write so much of the article that it gave the impression of having been written by a *Wallpaper* columnist. At that moment, I felt as though the captivity had reached its culmination in the achievement of a uniform diversity. "Senegal," wrote Jean-Marie Messier, in rock critic mode, "after having imported rap music, completely *Senegalized* it and transformed it into one of the most active and outspoken forms of local political expression . . . As for the electronic music that had its origin in Detroit, thanks to French DJs, it engendered the 'French Touch' that we dance to today . . . in Detroit." What can you do? Which way to the Egress? Is there a window left anywhere, in a corner even, to jump or vomit from?

Be subversive, dangerous, visionary, hostile, anarchist, punk, strung-out, whatever. "Destruction is cool," taught management guru Tom Peters in his book *The Circle of Innovation*. Such was the rhetoric of the economics of permanent revolution. You didn't even need to read books like Luc Boltanski and Ève Chiapello's *The New Spirit of Capitalism*.[28] You just had to open your eyes: United States, 1996. London, 1997. Paris, spring, 2000. The new economy is off and running. Welcome to cyberspace. Death to hierarchy. It was as though the spring of

1968 was being remarketed "New and Improved," and like that other spring, slogans didn't need billboards, but were written right on the walls. The slogans urged us to change the world, to recreate it according to our desires, to play as much as we wanted. Those who had read the American magazines from the west coast knew that one day or another, the springtime of the wired would soon reach the freeways of France. But who could have predicted its scope? The boosters were all ready. It was a perfect story, for didn't the new economic have its roots in the California counterculture? Didn't it all begin with hippies who listened to John Lennon, smoked joints, wore platform shoes and long hair, and dropped acid according to the teachings of Timothy Leary? That's where it all started, in the middle of the psychedelic era, a few miles from campuses overrun by student activists. That's where the founding fathers of e-commerce had begun their work. The media quickly drew their conclusions: the new economy reconciled insurrection and the spirit of free enterprise. "In the new universe, everything is possible because creativity, reactivity and flexibility are the new buzzwords."[29] Judging by the enthusiasm of the columnists in French newspapers, we were entering a utopia worthy of Fourier. *Openspace*, an architectural concept born in the squats that sheltered English punks in the 80s, now reappeared in more businesslike clothes as the idea behind internet incubators for young entrepreneurs. Quite naturally, the internet ate away at the last vestiges of authority. Management manuals reoriented themselves toward permanent revolution. There would no longer be any bosses, supervisors, inspectors or bureaucracies. What May 1968 failed to accomplish in the street, the web would deliver, and in the halls and boardrooms of commerce itself. We stepped boldly into the era of fulfilled anarchism, of a capitalism that knew neither God nor master—an economy without oppression. The business models of the new economy welcomed even the heresy of gratuity: a free connection to a world of services that cost nothing more than the willingness to put up with a bit of advertising on one's screen. In a few months, the New Spirit of capitalism forged in the Ivy League business schools of the West busted out onto the scene. While companies like Apple dug deep in their pockets to license the great icons of the counterculture— *El Ché*, Gandhi, Bob Dylan—for their ad spots, the figure of the ideal entrepreneur began to take shape: he had to be a rebel, a maverick, a superman. "For this, he must have intuition and talent, in the same sense we mean when we speak of artistic talent. His gaze sweeps across the world around him in search of new signs and he is always predicting, anticipating and sniffing out the links worth pursuing."[30]

Laughter from the Mud

Faced with the new captivity, there were at first only two options open to us: despair or laugh. I should add that in the beginning despair was the only option; laughter came later. You see, a man or a woman who grew up in the era of endings, who saw Situationism give itself up before the onrush of commodities, who saw their revolt put on sale in department stores—anyone who grows up in such circumstances and desires freedom can only begin their existence in despair. This is the state from which the children of the collapse are struggling to extricate themselves. For Naomi Klein, it's what made it necessary for her to write her book: "I spent a good part of my last

51

year in college discussing, with my best friend Lan Ying, the absurdity of living in a world where everything had already been done . . . We could leave the straight and narrow path of career materialism, but it was only to enter another narrow path—the road of the people who did not follow the road . . . Do you want to travel? Become a modern Jack Kerouac? Here's the *Let's Go Europe* path. You want to be a rebel? Avant garde artist? Go to the used bookstore and pick up your 'alternative' path, dusty, worm-eaten and worn down to the bone. Every place we could imagine changed before our eyes into a bundle of clichés—like in a Jeep ad or a standup comedy routine."[31]

Some will see in this despair the recurrent capriciousness of the spoiled children of the West, which History has so often condemned to boredom. "That nameless evil" that Serenus, the friend of Seneca, was unable to describe in the philosopher's *On Tranquility of Mind*. After all, a few weeks after the events of May 1968, didn't Pierre Viansson-Ponté write a piece in *Le Monde* entitled "France is Bored"? There was some truth to it. Boredom is a powerful catalyst of revolt. It has been ever since the French Revolution imposed the bourgeois ideal as the norm. And it will continue to be so for years to come: the delights and pleasures of capitalism are only capable of satisfying half our needs. It is only natural that the other half should occasionally awaken to remind us that in addition to our longing to possess lies a longing to be. But we were not there yet. Absent suicide, despair was for the time being the only viable option for us.[32]

Out of this despair came a burst of laughter. Initially, it became a weapon against guilt. It said: "Since there is nothing we can do about it, we might as well have a good time." And gradually, almost in spite of ourselves, the laughter replaced the despair. During this period—the beginning of the 90s—we chose laughter over freedom. It was the laughter of the vanquished, which unbeknownst to us was quietly filling our world with cynicism. "From radio to the press, from advertising to television channels, from boardrooms to coffeehouses, the same type of laughter has appeared almost everywhere—as a symbol, a guarantor and an expression of democracy,"[33] wrote Jean Paul Curnier. Make no mistake, we're not talking about a spontaneous explosion of joy. No, this laughter was born on the day after our funeral vigil, out of the ashes of ends. It was born as a defense against the two-headed memory of disillusion and horror, after the great abdication of power, and the dematerialization of the world . . . Yes, in that laughter pickled in the aesthetic of resignation, we heard the booming eulogy of human will and the thunderous applause that greeted the appearance of abdication on the stage. It was the laughter of the editors-in-chief who force feed us with outrageous facts and garnish them with snide little turns of phrase to emphasize that writing against one's times is completely pointless.

When I go back and try to pinpoint the first appearance of that laughter, a certain image always haunts me. Was it in Guatemala, in Honduras? An amazing spectacle. A sacred spectacle, par excellence. I was barely ten years old. It was on television. It was a little girl, right in front of the camera. Actually, it wasn't a little girl, it was a little girl's head, sticking up out of a mudpond, the rest of her body already submerged. The body already gone and the head too, vanishing. There, just a few yards from me, from us, from everyone. Thousands of miles away from everyone too. And the rescuers! Where were the rescuers? There were none. The only thing you could do was watch the little head of the little girl in the mud-pond. If I had to locate the source of that laughter, I'd look around that mudpond, even in the mud, in the spectacle of that mud. Because there too, suddenly, the image neutralized our outrage and laughter allowed us to bear our helplessness without dying of shame. Yes, we didn't kill ourselves on that day. Maybe we should have . . . out of dignity.

The laughter has changed since then. It's no longer a means of surviving despair. Now it is an instrument of submission. It is used incessantly to ridicule our dreams. I still remember those images from 1996, the ones that showed the "Intergalactic Conference" organized by Subcomandante Marcos. The TV news sought to prove its own relevance by showing the "behind the scenes" of the event, that was their "angle" on the story. Watching the media watching the media watching the media . . . The images showed a wall of cameras facing the head of the Zapatista Army, French intellectuals lost in the jungles of Lacandone, folklore and T-shirts bearing the image of the "Sub." The whole little demi-monde of global resistance wallowed in the mud. For there was mud there too. Mud around the huts, mud on the paths. There was unending heavy rain. The leaky roof let the rain in and mud filled the interior of the dormitories. Why was an area that furnished 40% of Mexico's hydro-electric power awash in mud within minutes of the first drops of rain? We might have asked ourselves that. Why in spite of huge oil and gas reserves did the building lack running water? Finally, why did that mud resemble the treatment reserved for the 10 million indians living in Mexico? Yes! We MIGHT HAVE . . . but no, we preferred another response, more modern, more Situationist, and admittedly, more conformist. What we saw was the farce of these intellectuals wallowing in the mud while the Zapatista uprising was *saved by 4x4s*. We got the message all right: misery is a spectacle. Oppression is an image. The little girl is in the mud. No one can help. It's the camera that's the problem. It's better to criticize the frame than what's inside it; at least the frame can be changed. You can't change the world. And anyway, like the angry queen said, "desiring revolt is already revolt." So that would be the angle: Marcos Superstar, and the Intergalactic Conference rained out. Just like Wimbledon. Very funny. That would make a nice punch line. We laugh in the editing room: pretty funny, those "I Love Marcos" T-shirts in the central market of San Cristóbal. "Did you see the American with the Ché Guevara pin? *Elle* called him a 'Fashion guerilla.'"

Seen through the humor of mass dandyism, the Zapatista uprising looks like a fall runway show. "It would seem as though Helmut Lang is trying to invent ski-mask style . . ." The whole world knows it. Nothing means anything. The entire world is in the mud, in the laughter of mud. "Chiapas is being bled through a thousand different channels: oil pipelines, gas pipelines, power lines, freight cars, through bank accounts, through trucks and pickups, boats and planes, secret trails, dirt roads, tracks and pathways; these lands continue to pay their tribute to various empires: oil, electric energy, cattle, money, coffee, bananas, honey, corn, cocoa, tobacco, sugar, soy, melons, sorghum, melons, mamey sapote, mangos, tamarind, avocados—and Chiapan blood flows out through 1,001 fangs sunk into the neck of southeastern Mexico. Billions of tons of natural resources go through Mexican ports, railway stations, airports, and road systems to various destinations: the United States, Canada, Holland, Germany, Italy, Japan—but all with the same destiny: to feed the empire. The dues that capitalism imposes on the southeast corner of the country ooze out, as they have since the beginning, in mud and blood."[34] What should we have heard in Marcos's words here? The story of capitalism's penetration of a remote backwater? A collection of cold statistics or rather the insurgent lyricism of a people cheated out of their life's blood, the funeral music of a wilderness converted into a system of commodity flows, of a primordial abundance pillaged by the logic of scarcity? The spectacle dismantled the world's reality, and with it went our capacity for outrage. We became little better than a studio audience for an unending performance. We were invited to submit our judgments, but as though we were film critics at a premiere. All the classic causes of revolt have now become raw materials themselves, commodities circulating through the same system, following the same routes as sorghum, tamarind and mangoes. They have Controlled Origin Labels and an exotic aftertaste.

If you want to understand *mass dandyism* in the era of the new captivity, start by imagining a man seated atop a pile of garbage, laughing. He knows each piece of trash in the pile by name; in fact, that's exactly what has set him off laughing. He can still be affected by *particular* things, but the sum of his experience with the world's objects has killed his desire to see things *in particular*. Not because he is blind—it's that he can't rid himself of the vision of the trash heap, which has made looking at things *in particular* seem pointless. He's no brute. On the contrary, he's a sensitive soul, feminine, incapable of violence. It's just that he's given up. If he's laughing, it's because he has *chosen* to live on the trash heap, and not against it. He's made it his home, his closet, his smoking room, and his study.

Laughter is his aesthetic . . . an aesthetic of resignation. Generally speaking, *mass dandyism* is not into evil. The idea of doing evil is repugnant to it, but at the same time it finds morality profoundly boring. It laughs out of principle, as a defense against the seriousness of those who want to teach it what it knows already. But from the top of its trash pile, it is often struck by a deep fatigue. Drunk with laughter, it stumbles on the idea that to sit *on top* of the garbage is also to be *part of* the garbage, and that by laughing so much it has actually *become* garbage. By becoming so familiar with mediocrity, *mass dandyism* has actually become mediocre *itself*. At first it only brushes against mediocrity, skirts it, avoids it, grazes it ever so slightly. Then it caresses it. Then . . . just a taste. Then it dives right in. Gets used to it. And so begins the period of getting rich . . . just to get rich. WITHOUT A MISSION. The memory of despair recedes and cynicism takes over completely. Brute calculation takes over from subtlety. Its denial continues a while longer, sometimes for an entire lifetime. Nevertheless, the last sparks of revolt sink below the waters and the cynical laughter flies ever higher, irresistible and resigned.

THE NEW STRANGLEHOLD
What is the color of water?

"*Young nomads, we love you! Be ever more modern, more mobile, more fluid . . . Be lighthearted, anonymous, precarious like drops of water or soap bubbles! For if you're not fluid, you'll become tacky real quick.*"[35]

"*The space of flows . . . is in the midst of becoming the dominant spatial manifestation of our societies . . . Advanced services, including finance, insurance, commercial real estate, legal services, advertising, industrial design, marketing, public relations, security . . . can all be considered as knowledge products and information flows.*"[36]

Like other inhabitants of the trendy neighborhoods of the New Architecture of the United World, the suffocating man was now a happy schizophrenic. The more the contradictory logic of information flows forced him to live a double life, the more he rejoiced. He was probably confusing his mild schizophrenia, his rootlessness, his nomadism and his freedom, but after all, the important thing was that he was filled with happiness. He loved the fact that he could live in two places at the same time. He thought of his happiness in terms of his electronic extensions. He thought of himself as a kind of human multimedia platform and was proud of it—to have a ear on the telephone, an eye on his email, a mouth on a lox sandwich and a foot on an airport escalator. He was even more proud of the fact that at the same moment, his other foot was crossing the aisles of an airliner en route across the Atlantic while his second eye took in a DVD. An MP3 file delivered up its contents into his other ear. The suffocating man liked to think that he was not really that mouth, nor those ears, nor that hand, nor those legs, nor the sum of all those parts of himself. He knew that he was downloadable, at least partially. Hadn't he sent an image of his sweaty neck and the sounds of his labored breathing to his squash teacher the last time he was on the court? He couldn't upload his BO, but OK, not a serious problem. He felt sufficiently disembodied.

From time to time, while traveling, he would contemplate his PDA. For him, it was not merely a simple list of acquaintances and contacts, but a veritable digital amplification of his being, a sort of cybernetic aura. At this point in his life, he was working seven days a week, twenty-four hours a day. Since he often traveled through many times zones, he would frequently find himself working more hours than actually existed in real-time.

One evening, for a change of pace he decided to drink a few glasses of champagne at an art opening on Paris's right bank. The invitation was a small masterpiece of chic minimalism. Grey on white with fine, spidery type and a single pink arrow showing the address and a date drawn in blocky pixels. At the opening, a doorman in beige gloves and a cosmonaut's suit hailed him, touching his hand to his helmet. Two DJs in fish costumes worked a bank of laptops, playing an aquatic symphony for marine mammals: ten hours of splashing, dolphin shrieks, and whale songs. The gallery was white and clinical. An intense light filled the space with a sense of weightlessness. Women's legs mounted on invisible pedestals seemed to hang in space. Protruding from the ceiling were dozens of hands and wrists covered with long gloves in cream-colored latex, groping in the void. Further along, a glass aquarium built into the wall displayed floating sections of a human brain. The water disappeared into a mantle of white foam. A hologram of a hippocampus trembled where it was projected, on a cloud of vapor. The show had an obscure title: "Licœur" The artist was attempting to represent the second phase of evolution. After having addressed accumulation, his attention had turned to liquefaction. "Man is 65% water," one read on the installation program. "Information makes us flow as surely as we make it flow. 'Licœur' attempts to trace the intersections of technology, intelligence and the aquatic."

The title had come to him while drinking a cognac on the top floor of the Marriott in New York City. Watching the giant screens crawling with stock information from the NASDAQ, he felt the intoxication of liquidity, the vertigo of his exploded, dismantled body as it was taken inside the network of the New Architecture of the United

World. All he needed to do then was follow his intuition: the world wants to flow out, to be freed from the dimension of bodies. Form, he felt, was leaving the three spatial dimensions behind, manifesting only through movement, streaming, traveling. As a professional, he knew he had to embrace a new aesthetic, one inspired by the interconnections of waterways, an aquatic ecosystem of information in which each sense and each limb was autonomous.

Mostly, the opening of "Licœur" filled the suffocating man with a terrible nausea. He realized all of a sudden that avant-garde art had adopted the reigning criteria of information-age capitalism. And he saw that in his happy schizophrenia, he too had accepted the same fluid dream. Looking around him, he saw that the opening had drawn an extraordinarily diverse crowd: corporate CEOs, underground icons, film stars, politicians, artists, designers, and cyberpunk pundits. Amidst the whisperings and snide remarks without which art openings would not be art openings, he caught a bit of the spirit of the times: "What would be really cool would be to cover yourself with scales and swim upriver like a salmon stuffed full of antibiotics!" enthused a woman in a half-Geisha, half-Andalusian outfit. "My next body mod is going to be to get a genital implant for cybersex stimulation," declared one ordinary human to his even more ordinary neighbor. The only sane comment he overheard was something to the extent that it was a shame there was nothing to drink at the opening of an installation entitled 'Licœur.' The rest of the conversation was just euphoric murmuring on the theme of liquefaction. "No, really, I think he's right. The future is going to be liquid. Take me for example, tonight I'm in Paris, tomorrow I'll be in Tokyo, then New York. Meanwhile I'm sending last-minute details for the current collection to Milan. It's all about water."

The suffocating man was in no mood to discuss it. Pretending to ponder the misty hologram of the hippocampus, he eavesdropped on the conversation of an over exuberant brunette, who was introducing herself to another person as the sponsor's communications rep. The sponsor was a brand of aperitif, Ricard-Licœur. The brunette went on about how she had helped turn this working-class booze into the flavor of the month for the global smart set. "Solidity, my dear, is totally fifteen minutes ago," she said. "Fluidity, on the other hand, is like culture meets economics and falls in love. Listen. That's a dolphin singing . . ." She stopped in mid-sentence and began to wiggle her ass to the music. The fish-costumed DJs began to run the ocean sounds through a reverb and the songs of the whales and dolphins morphed into a sweet funky beat. The second half of their piece began— a set of aquatic lounge music.

"They can't stand their bodies," the suffocating man thought. "Any bodies. Time and space are over. The meat, its skin, its guts, over. Substance, matter, stuff, all gone. Welcome to a world without menstruation. Get with the style of the times, boyo. Forget about territory. Time is where it's all happening." He suddenly had a clearer idea of what it was that was keeping him from breathing.

In the days that followed he had trouble concentrating. To his officemates, it was plain that he was struggling against some unseen obstacle. They all worked together in a warehouse-style openspace, all raw concrete and steel. From their desks, they watched as he held long conversations with no one in particular. Of course, insanity was no longer a problem. On the contrary, it was encouraged and even considered a mark of dynamism, the key quality of a dot-com entrepreneur.

Well, sort of. The truth is that his monologues were becoming bizarre enough to worry some of his colleagues. "I will be the rock amidst the roiling waters," he intoned. "My body is heavy. My fingers will be hedgerows. In the age of real-time, I will remain immobile." Over by the espresso machine, where the continual hiss of steam covered voices, rumors began to develop. "He's been saying 'heavy' over and over since he came in . . . dude's fried some wires somewhere, that's for sure . . . in his brain . . . in the bathroom, he kept singing 'I'm so fat, I'm so huge, sooo huge,' like 'I'm the Great Wall of China!' and shit, then he goes 'Go fuck yourself, agents of the great liquidation. I'm not afraid of you, I'm immobile, immobile.'"

The suffocating man figured he knew what relativity was: when the abscissas and ordinates of everything moves, only a still point gives motion any meaning. So from this he concluded that soon the trend would reverse. The representatives of the masses, of matter, static beings, the immobile ones, yes! they were the new avant garde. Not long after this revelation he received his pink slip. He had gotten a little too "out there" for his company. Even his old friends were afraid of being seen with him. He had chosen the sedentary camp against the nomads. Now (they said) he was a loser, a reactionary, even.

There was a certain irony to getting fired. The suffocating man had never signed a contract. He had been part of the early sweat equity crew, workers who gave up job security by choice—a group of privileged young dandies who had rallied behind the idea of "Absolute Risk," what they thought was a "revolutionary" conception of society, one with no welfare or insurance, public or private. Under Absolute Risk, the commandment "Thou *shalt not insure" would be the supreme dogma, enforced with the goal of recreating a pre-bourgeois man, with no safety net, naked, in direct contact with his destiny. This was to take place on the one hand by maximizing encounters with risk and chance, with accident, and on the other, by reawakening the primal instincts, once they had been extricated from the gigantic mess of guarantees and insurance that had smothered them.*

Now that he was on his own, cast out, without a dime and reduced to panhandling to get by, the suffocating man had all the time in the world to retrace the intellectual journey that had brought him so far, and so to begin his long voyage across the digital desert.

All throughout my adolescence, I was torn between two forms of dissent, one artistic and the other social.[37] The first was characterized by a hatred of anything bourgeois—their conventions, their savings, their creature comforts. Its posture was aristocratic; it celebrated idleness. To the rational arrangement of life, it opposed the eruption of irrationality and the beauty of the bizarre. The radical *no* that it articulated in so many different ways linked the poetry of Baudelaire, the magnetic fields of Lautréamont, the nonchalance of Rimbaud, Dada craziness, surrealism, the Situationist diaspora, and the negativity of punk rock. Social critique could never allow itself the luxury of this wholesale rejection of society. From the early days of the industrial revolution, it generally limited itself to modest reforms and spent more time binding the wounds of the workers than it did spitting in the face of the middle class. It was inclined to compromise, to realism. From my window in the Paris's Latin Quarter, I watched them, body after body, one union after another as they marched towards the ministry buildings. The artistic critique was seductive and sensual, but on the other hand the complacency of the art world always drew me back to the dignity of the underprivileged. I dressed up for the first and dressed down for the second, always going back and forth. Simple and raw during the day, sophisticated and snide at night, when I'd transform from partisan to dandy. First modest, then extroverted. First humble, then condescending. Rebellious, then jaded. The cities of the world had taught me urbanity and subtlety. My flesh, and maybe also the vestiges of the religion that had been shoved down my throat as a child, brought me back to the way of materialism. I longed to reconcile these two approaches and in so doing rid myself of this inner division. But as the century approached its end, I felt that the gap was only widening. The spirit of revolt itself was being torn apart. In the polite conversation of the 90s, just uttering the words "politics," "territory," or "social" was enough to tag one as a conservative. The dimension of bodies, the inertia of societies, the whole range of the physical and the incarnate was now considered tiresome and archaic. One had to be light, to ride on the wind. "But one day, perhaps, this century will be Deleuzian," Foucault once said. His tentative prediction had abruptly come to pass.[38]

Right up until the beginning of the 80s, there was an overlap between the two critiques. In *The New Spirit of Capitalism*, Boltanski and Chiapello cite the example of the journal founded by Sartre, *Les Temps Modernes*, which "took care . . . to reconcile the proletarianism of the Communist Party with the libertinism of the artistic avant garde."[39] One word authorized this alliance: TRANSGRESSION: "Workers locking up their boss, homosexuals embracing in public or artists exhibiting trivial objects removed from their workaday context and placed in a gallery or in a museum—in each case, what was behind such gestures were different forms of the same TRANSGRESSION of the bourgeois order."[40] Artists and workers made a unified front, held together by outrage. In Paris, the philosophers of the time created a sort of under-ground railway between Saint-Germain-des-Prés and working-class neighborhoods like Boulogne-Billancourt. They wrenched art from art history and thrust it into the machine grease. Such efforts were not always welcomed, but for the most part they worked. Communications were established between all the transgressors of norms. The JUST had a mouthpiece and a presence. It had its own poetry, its tribunes, rhymes, slogans, and an avant-garde with two hearts: aesthetic and revolutionary.

I witnessed the end of this alliance. It resembled a great departure, a momentous setting-off on a momentous voyage. Hurry up, hurry up, one seemed to hear, we're taking off! The artists didn't even pause to take out their handkerchiefs; they left land behind them without a second thought, without a twinge of remorse. I've still got one foot on the pier and one on the deck. Like Damiens, the French regicide whose story begins *Discipline and Punish*, I feel drawn and quartered, I feel the cartilage in my groin ripping apart as aesthetics and politics continue to diverge. No one tore at my breast with iron tongs. There was no executioner burning me beforehand with molten sulphur. I am neither guilty nor condemned—it's the spirit of the times we live in that's tearing me apart, the fucked-up blackmail of these times. The desire for diversity has eclipsed the fire of transgression. The elites have been mesmerized by their fluid ideal, and the intellectuals have abandoned the earthiness of the indigent for higher spheres. The poets have missed their calling. Philosophers are more and more rare, and the indictment of people like Sartre has created a justification for detachment. All that remains of the spirit of revolt are annoying, fossilized slogans, the gross sentimentality of the complainers, and the poor bodies of the poor. So, are you coming? You have to choose, my friend. Coming aboard? Yes or no? Out there is the open ocean, the cybernetic seas. Here is only sad and dried-up dirt. I can tell that you are a man of the times, why don't you follow your destiny? You've got a good education. Technology is no mystery to you. You'll be useful to us. And well paid. And anyway, why stay here? Soon there'll be nothing left but rusting factories, temp jobs, and illegal aliens forced to wander from place to place forever. If you have to be a nomad, it's better to be one by choice, right? All of us who are going, you'll see, they're great guys. If you can put your intelligence at their disposal, and God knows they need intelligence, they'll make you filthy rich. Well? Obviously, I wanted to get on board. Because I wasn't even twenty yet, and when you're not even twenty yet, you certainly don't want to already be too old to be a part of the spirit of your times. And after all, the spirit of the times was working for me. It was feeding me. Capitalism wants you when you're young—fresh blood, someone who knows what the kids are thinking, has a feeling for the times. But if I were to get on board, I'd have to leave revolt behind. You don't bite the hand that feeds you. Sorry, I don't think so . . . maybe that's what they were calling the death of the counterculture, this huge boat sailing on the empty air, weighing anchor and setting off full of hand-biters for a long cruise through the reefless lagoons of the digital ocean.

Trying to explain this inner division, I remembered a book that had received a lot of attention during the period between the two world wars. *The Treason of the Intellectuals* was written by Julien Benda, a French essayist who left little else to posterity besides this accusatory pamphlet and a few introductions added to later editions to underline how right he had been. Towards the end of the 19th century, Benda argued, the mind abandoned its duties. The intellectuals—the philosophers and the great minds of the time—had failed in their mission. They had abandoned universal values and become little more than the credentialed whores of secular passions. Turning their back on ideas that began with capital letters—Justice, Truth, Peace, Reason—they had signed on to the venal agendas of the rat race. Right up in front in the group portrait of the traitors were the apologists of the National Idea, the pundits who had ranted on about the glory and greatness of the Fatherland. Benda had grown up during World War I. He had watched as the nationalist pride of the European peoples swelled towards disaster. He had watched as the war of words between France and Germany over the disputed territory of Alsace-Lorraine grew hot, as Italian poets and painters prostituted their artistic prowess in the service of national unity, as English writers fretted over the decline of the British Imperium. In the first edition of his book, published in 1927, he also denounced those trying to stoke the flames of the class struggle in Russia, in Germany, in the libraries of Parisian universities.[41] Across the four corners of the Old Continent, men of letters were wearing out their fine fountain pens with calls for bloodshed. Proletarians against bourgeois. Marxists against social democrats. It was a passion different from that of the nationalists, but treason all the same. Everywhere, Benda saw intellectuals' eagerness to become part of History and set it on fire. While others looked into the flames and saw political commitment as mandatory for the intellectual,[42] Benda, like a jealous husband enraged at the spectacle of so many metaphysical adulteries, kept to his inventory of errors and deceptions.

During the 90s, a similar movement led intelligence to what was this time not an intellectual betrayal but a treason of the flesh. Four tiny drops of water squeezed out to dissolve the last bastions of resistance. A drop of science fiction to prepare the heirs of the protest movements of the past for the era of biotechnology. A drop of *subverted* Deleuze and Guattari to recreate man in the image of singularities and flows. A drop of sweat to transform the night and its trances into a space for business networking. Finally, a weightless economy, creative and speculative, as recompense for this betrayal. So many drops in a permanent IV drip that has transformed the body until it is no longer the cradle of revolt, but a unit of body-capital, deterritorialized, rootless, free from the constraints of time and space. A packet of information in a sea of the same, a conductor, and no longer a site of resistance. That's where one should look to explain the dissociation of aesthetics and politics, of intelligence and labor, of modernity and the incarnation. For how else, apart from this transformation, can one explain the new condescension with which intellectuals are treating the material world?

Ascetics, Piss, Cyborgs

I dug deep in search of an explanation for this betrayal. I sifted through my memories. I once had three pictures tacked to the wall at my bedside. The first was by Picasso, from the blue period, then one by El Greco, and finally an engraving by Emil Nolde. I had removed the other images to leave only these three insane, emaciated, hollow-cheeked faces. It was a way of telling myself that my childhood was over.

At fifteen, I had adopted a regimen of abstinence, renunciation, light anorexia, and heavy underlining of all the books that were not on the reading list. Picture me wearing a beige suede jacket, oblong glasses, and an expression indicating contempt for all the things men are generally interested in, contempt for cars, for life insurance, for family, sex, family, business, sports, fashion, family, TV, routine, money, family. I have just learned that my rhesus factor is O+, allowing me to announce at every occasion that I am *zero positive*, and thus oppressed, a carrier of the gay disease. My parents don't understand—and how could I explain it to them—I am depressed *not to be sick*. I try harder. *Zero positive, seropositive*, this is my claim to victimhood, my discrimination, the affliction that will give me the legitimacy I crave and allow me to class myself among the deviants, the pariahs, the outcasts. I try harder. A few yards from my mattress, like a hole in the wall, the three faces of Picasso, El Greco, and Nolde are there to give shape to my dawning awareness of the rebel body; they become expressions of its first avatar, the ascetic. To this being of refusal, to this worn form, I attribute every virtue: sobriety, so rare around me, isolation and poverty, the only way to face the reign of abundance. At the other end of my room is a sort of lump that had escaped my purge of the premises. It lies there, pointless, with its styrofoam beads and its leather envelope split open, the absolute opposite of the ascetic—a furniture object destined to be worn out, thrown out, one of the small victories of soft society. Each time friends plopped down on it, I watched it spread out beneath them, precisely molding their bodies according to their weight and shape. It mimicked the give and take of flesh itself. The soft crunching of the styrofoam beads seemed like a metaphor in itself: the beanbag! Bold new creation of Western Man, a turning point of civilization. Under the pretext of liberating bodies from the old constraints, this great achievement of design dissolves them into a formless mass. See for yourself: women, dogs, children, anyone who sinks into a beanbag soon enough loses their essence. The specific qualities of the beanbag-user's body are submerged and scrambled,

replaced with a vague larva-like form, a molluscoid aesthetic, a vegetative ideal. Ascetics resist such aberrations.
They are the keepers of a secret. Their faces, tormented
like Artaud's, seem twisted in the same shriek. Against
the double oppression of flows, they demand that the
flesh *howl* and the flux explode from *within*. They confront the juices of power, the secretions of production,
the flows of capital rushing in from the outside with the
sluggish rivers of the bowels, the streaming of piss, the
flows of shit and sperm. This howling stirs something in
me. Artaud had a name for it: he called it the "the body
without organs." For me, it's an image of perfect resistance, where each pixel of the epidermis goes to war
against the double machine of industry and desire.

I didn't spend very long as an ascetic. "Hormones
have reasons that reason know nothing of," my doctor
explained to me, borrowing a phrase from one of Pascal's
most banal *pensées*. Sex was doing its secret work, leading me towards another incarnation of the dissident
body, the same profane, obscene being of shit and piss
and sperm and water that Artaud wrote of. The revolt of
the flesh is not taught in classrooms—you have to do it
yourself. So somewhat clumsily, I traced the history of
this body with my own. I cross-dressed, I acted like I
thought whores acted, adopting a look that was a
watered-down caricature of the 20s, complete with long
cigarette holder. I thought of the cubists as the first
deconstructionists—they had demolished perspective,
and with it the view of a way out. They had learned from
psychoanalysis to find a source of interior inspiration
that was neither soul nor reason. An it, an id, a residue
of the perversions of childhood, a war machine that
could be turned on the bourgeois order. I discovered the
centrifuged faces of Bacon. I admired Genet's *Carolines*,

those heroic faggots who braved the high society of the *Ramblas* in Barcelona to leave flowers at the *pissoirs* where they had their liaisons. "A group of faggots numbered about thirty, I saw them go by and tagged along a safe distance behind. I knew that my place was among them, not because I was one of them, but because of the acid in their voices, their cries, their outrageous gestures which had no other purpose, it seemed to me, than to attempt to go farther in attracting the world's contempt. The Carolines had greatness. They were the Women of Shame."[43] Very quickly, I left the boiling piss of Genet for the *eye* of Bataille.[44] "Piss on me, piss on my ass . . . she repeated with a kind of thirst."[45] I experimented with the scandalous and ambiguous bodies of TVs and TGs. I discovered the experiments of the Viennese *Aktionistes* and their forbidden plunges into the carcasses of disemboweled animals. I got drunk in the cabarets of Lautrec. For long hours I leafed through issues of *Bizarre*, John Alexander Coutts' S&M magazine.

And so I found my way along this archipelago of taboos. One word led to another and on and on. "The beautiful is always bizarre," wrote Baudelaire, opening up the 19th century to me so that I could encounter Sacher-Masoch, the namesake of masochism—the second term of perversity's equation: Sacher-Masoch, the theorist of pain inverted and transformed into pleasure, and the private contract taken to the extremes of its internal logic. When dissident bodies demand the right to damage one another by mutual consent, the authorities are right to sound the alarm. I stopped off in California, in the midst of its S&M community, as a matter of fact. Elvis was still alive, I was not yet born. I met up with the *Modern Primitives*, still just in a book, and a window opened, leading me into the back rooms of San

Francisco restaurants. The performances that took place there gave the aesthetic canon of the West a run for its money. Challenging the taboos against body marking, they celebrated tattooing, scarifications, suspension by hooks. A thin red stream of TRANSGRESSION ran down the walls.

I had opted for the path of the ascetic out of pure intuition. I explored the unnamable. I incarnated myself in the two bodies of asceticism, the body without organs and the desiring machine, and from these incarnations I grasped that for the artist and the writer they were sites where resistance could find expression. Instruments, weapons for inflicting shock. But these days they shock no one. For the understudies who are now leading these extravaganzas of infamy have abandoned the flesh. By the middle of the 90s, the prefix *trans-* no longer suggested TRANSGRESSION, but rather TRANSFORMATION, CONNECTION, HYBRIDIZATION. You no longer cut into your skin to *épater les bourgeois*, to scandalize the values of the West; now you did it to help embody its futurist dreams. You no longer imbibed draughts of excrement and ejaculate, you injected information. The ascetic and the unnamable betrayed us. I watched as they became infatuated with the electronic flux, and in return, the flux demanded total surrender. The flux ordered them not only to accept capitalism, but to desire it. "What's modern is good. What's fluid is modern. Thus, what's fluid is good." They bowed to the logic of this syllogism. All hail the great flux, gentlemen! Goodbye dissident bodies. Idiotically misreading Deleuze and Guattari, they made a dogma out of the ideas set forth in *Anti-Œdipus*, betraying its spirit completely. This betrayal is likely the effect of a perverse trade-off: "But what is the revolutionary path? Is there one? Abandoning the world market . . ?

Or might the path not be to go in the opposite direction? Go farther, that is to say, farther in the same direction that the market is going, in the direction of decoding and deterritorialization?"[46] This "farther" is where we live today, today when the dissident body has embraced capital's ideal.

I watched as the symptoms of this betrayal overran the avant-garde like an epidemic of botulism. One machine after another, organ after organ. 1999. In Williamsburg, Brooklyn, where open-mouthed hangars still confront Manhattan from across the East River, I went see a show by Pan-Sonic,[47] a duo of electronic musicians with a reputation sufficient to attract the attention of this colony of New York artists. The venue was a blandly impersonal concert hall. They served lousy beer and the sounds amounted to little more than clusters of extreme samples spurting from two laptops. A few minutes before the concert I interviewed the two musicians. They were not very talkative. "We're into machines that run amok," was about all I got out of them. Visibly annoyed, a local art critic with intellectual-looking horn-rims listened to the interview. Picking up that I was French, he couldn't help giving me a piece of advice . . . philosophical advice. "Traditionally," he began, "we think of the body as a system of organs, each with their own specific function. Pan-Sonic's music is not about that kind of body. No, no. Their music is struggling to give birth to the body as defined by Artaud, Deleuze, and Guattari. To listen to Pan-Sonic is to experience disincarnation. It's the sound of deterritorialization."[48] It was all I could do to keep from laughing. What would the body without organs be doing there, so disembodied, so far from its own howls? I didn't bother to ask. I suppose he was completely within his role of as a cultural critic, after all, the palaver of cultural critics is a wonderful register of the manias of the times. As it happened, that was indeed where we were, culturally speaking, right smack in the middle of the time of disincarnation and dismemberment. All I had to do was listen, and soon I would no longer feel anything. Goodbye space, hello speed.

Somewhat earlier in the day I had made a visit to Fakeshop, once a collective of young researchers, now disbanded. And as a matter of fact, the performance piece they were preparing was on the theme of the body without organs. The entry to their space was an array of sheets of corrugated aluminum. On a circular bench, performers stared into surveillance cameras, and their pupils were projected on screens directly opposite them. That the body without organs should be so ubiquitous was more than just a New York trend. This body—a *wired* body without organs, more precisely—was being dreamt of everywhere. Its disciples adopted the ideas of Artaud not for the spirit of revolt they exemplified, but for the technological fusion they made possible. There was nothing anachronistic about enlisting a surrealist from the 20s in this project. Absolutely not, said the zeitgeist. The body without organs was the anticipation of the flesh-interface, the prefiguration of flatscreen man.

Two weeks earlier in Paris, I had had a long discussion with Luka Zpira, a cyberpunk performer who had six polytetrafluorethyelene balls implanted in his solar plexus. He had founded a body modification laboratory in Avignon in the south of France called *Body-Art*. It was a sort of mothership where the little community of European mutants came to do their biomechanical shopping. I met Zpira in a room at the Ibis Hotel near the Bastille in Paris. He wore shoes that made Creepers look like humble wingtips—their Giant Robot-style soles were eight-inches thick, impossible to find in stores. I had just come in when I noticed that he had cued up a piece of ambient music as if to welcome me to a kind of temporary cyberspace created in the hotel room for my visit. "My modification began in my mind. I went through a really self-destructive period, I was a punk rocker, et cetera. And if I was going to survive, I needed something to live for. I started out with a tattoo on my arm and the shoulder, but my first real mutation were the implants in my torso and then when I had the chrome-cobalt teeth put in. What I would love to be able to do now is to apply technologies to my body in order to no longer be a slave to the machine." Pure delusion! So this is what punk ends up leading to? Luka was the living proof of Greil Marcus's complete blindness—the trail blazed by Johnny Rotten and Sid Vicious led not to Dada but to DATA. From the watershed moment of punk in the 70s, all Marcus retained was the gesture of negation: "There were no more coats, so people began to dress in rips and holes, safety pins and staples through the flesh as well as cloth, to wrap their legs in plastic bin liners and trash bags, to drape their shoulders in remnants of curtains and couch coverings left on the street longer any coats, so people started wearing rips and holes, with safety pins and staples through their skin as well as through their clothes . . . There was a reversal of perspectives, of values: a sense that anything was possible, a truth that could only be proven only by the negative. What had been good—love, money, and health—was now bad. What had been bad—hate, panhandling, and disease—now was good."[49] Since the 80s, the raging bodies of punk—at least the ones that had survived, had learned their science-fiction lessons: I am you are we are all information. The body is information. Biology hooks into the mechanical. The two realms melt into one. There is no more ego, no more id, no superego, just organic and technological machines and the interconnections between them. It was an escape worthy of the self-destructive impulses of the escapees. Format C love: this download without control-alt will delete all our future downloads—C is the virus that is now staphing our networked slaughter—hypertexts leave us perplexed—plex—plex—plexication of our itera- tions—will we retrovirus one day? I print an S—prints S—prints S—and hope to informat C love without limits there is no not coming back—Our immunologic is mean- ingless so why don't we flow in and drink-yes-drink-to- our-dissolution.

William Gibson's books had something to do with it. The work of this cyberpunk master left in its wake a fully-imagined system of magic wiring and matrix con- nections, one of the subtle preconditions for the consum- mation of the digital age. Gibson conquered dissident bodies—he hurled them to the ground with such force that nothing was left but a bunch of 19" monitors. What *Neuromancer* evoked was less negation by safety pin than the world of implanted technology. Inside, you dis- covered a gallery of posthuman clichés where the barmen were equipped with prostheses and the girls resembled cable networks. "Ratz presided over the bar, with his artificial arm that tapped out a monotonous rhythm to fill the Kirin glasses."[50] And then . . . "She was twenty years old. New lines of pain were beginning to deepen, permanently, at the corner of her mouth. Her brown hair was drawn back by a band of printed silk. The pattern might have represented a printed circuit or the layout of a city."[51] *Neuromancer* was a perfect representation of the period's rampant condescension for the body. "In the bars he frequented [Case, the hero] during his glory days, the elitist attitude demanded a certain contempt for the flesh. The body was a piece of meat."[52] And meanwhile I was listening to literati and art critics say the same things . . . it was curious how it all came together. Gibson's future was my present. Contempt for "the meat" was no longer a dream of science fiction, for the members of the intellectual demi-monde it was the trendiest of fashionable ideas. Now this attitude was no longer denounced as a form of resentment, it was glorified by a kind of chic Nietzscheism, vacuous and technofetishist.[53] "He remembered the smell of his skin in the overheated darkness of a coffin near the port, felt the fingers clawing the small of his back. He thought: always the meat with the meat's demands."[54] Case has just finished fucking Mona. I wrapped up my visit with Luka Zpira. The counterculture and the avant-garde began to sing once more in unison, a song with a strange lilt to it. Let us dissolve ourselves in the great cybernetic flux. Let's leave reality behind.[55]

Flux is Chix

There is another painting that is emblematic of this betrayal. It's not by Picasso, El Greco, or Bacon. I never put it up on my wall. I never loved it like I loved the ascetics and the unnamable bodies, my archipelago of taboos. It is a 1954 picture by Richard Lindner called *Boy with Machine*. This picture shows a teenager in short pants, baby fat still on his face, his torso moored to the ground by two enormous, hamlike thighs, the entire figure embroiled in the gears of a powerful machine that bristles with screws and cranks. A stock of fresh meat rolling towards the chopper of an industrial assembly line. *Boy with Machine* is also the image that opens *Anti-Œdipus*. Deleuze and Guattari describe the picture in these terms: "A huge, turgid child, having been hooked up, making one of his little desiring machines work, on top of a huge social technical machine."[56] The remarkable characteristic of this turgid child, though Deleuze and Guattari say nothing about it, is that he is smiling. A strange faraway smile, a smile that announced that the duel between body and the machine was over. Soon, the body will no longer be proletarian. It will no longer suffer the strain of labor or have to endure the servitude of capital. The turgid child smiles because he has understood something that his contemporaries never even caught a glimpse of. He knew—and his obesity bore witness to this illumination—he knew that he himself was a machine criss-crossed by flux, porous, open at each end. Behold! Here is a man who is neither an ascetic, nor a trans-, nor upside-down, nor infamous, nor dissident, but merely a machine among machines among machines among machines, a user, recorder, producer, from mouth to sphincters. "And so the anus-machine is connected to the intestine-machine, the intestine-machine to the stomach-machine, the stomach machine to the mouth-machine . . . Pockets of water and kidney stones; flows of hair, flows of drool, flows of sperm, shit or piss produced by partial objects, constantly intersected by other partial objects, which give rise to other flows that are taken up by other partial objects . . . Probably, each organ-machine interprets the whole world according to its own flows, based on the energy that flows from it."[57]

In spite of itself, *Anti-Oedipus* made flows hip. Is there a better parallel than this mechanical incantation of the body renouncing its integrity to the point where it sees itself only as a sum of transforming organs? "Capital is in fact the capitalist's body without organs, or rather the capitalist being's body without organs. But as such, it is not only the fluid and petrified substance of money, to the sterility of money it will lend the form under which the body produces money. It produces surplus value as the body without organs reproduces itself, flourishes and stretches out to the ends of the universe."[58] It would probably be completely misunderstanding the work of Deleuze and Guattari to find in it an apology for capitalism. That said however, it's not completely unheard of for the posterity of a work to be founded on a misreading. "There is no important idea that stupidity can't quickly find out how to make use of," wrote Robert Musil. I can vouch for that. Citation after citation, once the world was chewing on it, the meaning of the pair's critical monument grew more and more distorted. As soon as the flows of capital were linked to the handsome Antonin, the madman, the rebel, surrealism's stowaway, the royal road to misreading was laid open. Money became seen a sort of victim, tormented by trade barriers that sought to confine it. The body had been liberated; now it was capital's turn. We had done away with the corset, now financial markets had to be freed from their restraints. It was glamorous. Capital became glamorous. Sexy, à la mode, trendy. It suddenly appeared in new clothes, was suddenly fabulous. Its new face was dazzling and fresh. It had a darling figure and adorable rosy cheeks. And those eyes! Just take a look at those eyes! Simply marvelous! Even the story was beautiful. Deleuze and Guattari were not merely philosophers, they were fantastic storytellers. Genuinely gifted. Real writers, by God! Listen to the rhythm, the cadence: "It produces surplus value as the body without organs reproduces itself, flourishes and stretches out to the ends of the universe."[59] The Word makes more converts than all the philosophers of the world put together, and what a powerful word it was. No one had any idea what it meant, but that was hardly important. The gist of it was clear: those who accept the joys flowing from the liberated body have no right to condemn the liberation of capital flows. If they do they're denying a part of themselves. Besides Artaud, *Anti-Œdipus* retroactively recruited many other figures and placed them in the service of its program. It quoted the best. Henry Miller for starters, the ogre, the outlaw, the force of nature from Rome, New York. One more writer that Europe had elevated from bum to dharma bum, from obscene scribbler to great writer. One has to admire the Old World's talent for that type of thing, the goodwill that it has always shown to cursed outsiders: "I love everything that flows, even the menstrual flow that carries away the seed unfecund . . . and my guts spill out in a grand schizophrenic rush, an evacuation that leaves me face to face with the absolute."[60] The absolute, the limits of the universe, menstrual flows and capital flows, financial orgasm. Desire is a flow. Love desire. Love flows. Desire the economy of desire. Desire your flows and those of the other! Drink your piss, get rich. Lick yourself. Suck off men and women. Suck their beings and their belongings without distinction. And this stock market, give it to me so that I can knead its shares in my hands, so that I can caress them, play with them, enjoy them.

When *Anti-Œdipus* was first published, in 1972, open conflict was still possible. The ascetic—the body without organs—was still fighting. It rejected the world of flows. On its side of the battle lines stood the unnamable body

of the trans-, the travs-, the inverted, and the monsters—
a desiring machine, crossing swords with the forces of
morality.[61] That was then. Before the *dematerialized*
economy, the network economy had replaced the economy of heavy industry and raw materials. Before managers, consultants, business school students, artists,
admen, critics, journalists, philosophers, human
resource directors, department managers and product
managers, researchers, investors, and consumers drank
the hemlock of *informational capitalism*. I say hemlock
not so much to suggest that it was a poison, but rather
because like hemlock, the information society makes the
body gradually go numb. From my philosophy studies, I
had at least retained this: "Today: THE DEATH OF
SOCRATES." Another memory. Words on a blackboard
from my first year at high school, the Lycée Henri IV.
The seating in the lecture hall is steeply raked. It seems
that this is a school where we train the elite, which is
good, because I'm very elitist. Very quickly, I learn that
the only relationship between the two terms is an ety-
mological one. The elite are with few exceptions disap-
pointing, mediocre, and vulgar. They have nothing to
do with the sublime, with elegance or dignity—those
pearls lost in a tangle of seaweed. The specter of the
dead philosopher Althusser hovers over the school's
courtyard, giving the sun a morose, Marxist tint. We are
seated two per desk. Grafitti tags are carved into the
wooden desktops. *Love from X to Y/Beer makes you
piss/What's the difference between all or nothing/Vote
Socialist*. The students are silent. They're as dumb here
as they are anywhere else. The steam on the windows
says winter. Outside, some friends are playing basketball.
I know the teacher is the author of an important book
on the relationship between philosophy and painting.

He uses striking images when he talks, like: "Rugby is a good metaphor for education because in rugby you advance by making backwards passes. Soccer isn't a metaphor for anything." He has interesting theories, like this one: "The birth of perspective paved the way for the Cartesian 'I' and the emergence of the SUBJECT by indicating that there is only a single point from which one can observe a painting." Sometimes he gets a little sad: "Pascal's writings borrow from the genre of the *Vanitas*: life is obsessed with death like a skull that seems to stare at you." As for the lesson on THE DEATH OF SOCRATES, what stayed with me was the description of how after swallowing the poison, first the philosopher's feet grew cold, then his calves, then his thighs, his hips, his belly, his chest, his heart, and so on, until finally the soul itself had also become senseless. The hemlock of the flux-body has a similar effect; it produces a strange intoxication in which *technologically* advanced beings forget not only their own incarnation—which I could care less about—but also are led to deny the incarnation of others.[62]

I especially remember one expression I'd keep hearing wherever I went. Its resonance in the narrow circles of global hipsterdom seemed to grow stronger every day. New York, London, Paris, Tokyo, Milan, Barcelona. "I'm so schizo—Skeeze! You say skeeze. Not schizo. Schizo is *so* 15 minutes ago. *Skeeze! Skeeze!* Get it?" I can't say how many times that ridiculous little word burned my ears. In English, in French, in Italian, in Spanish. It was never uttered without some hint of satisfaction, with the snide little smile of voluntary slaves. The suggestion was that yes, one was completely overloaded, and proud of it. Modern living, you know.

Working three jobs at once. Permanent—and expected—job insecurity. Job insecurity turned against itself. That phrase I heard from a harried businessman in Kuala Lumpur, a film critic before and after a film, an art director a few days before they put the current number of the magazine to bed, an actor who claimed that he was always between two films, between two roles, between two girlfriends, between two selves. For the *skeeze*, it was important to be a nomad without ever getting homesick. Always living for the immediate future, never for the present. For the *skeeze*, the thing was to have versions of oneself scattered all over the place. Recorded earlier in one place, live in another. The *skeeze* was the symptom of the spirit's dilution in the era of the fluid body. It was not the same thing as schizophrenia, a clinical designation. For the liquefied art-capitalist elite *Skeeze* was another name for happiness. Those who had read *Anti-Œdipus* had no reason to be surprised. Deleuze and Guattari had anticipated everything. In fact, it was the heart of their book. "The schizophrenic deliberately seeks out the very limit of capitalism: he is its inherent tendency brought to fulfillment, its surplus product, its proletariat, and its exterminating angel."[63] Thirty years later, people were saying *skeeze* instead of schizo and it no longer had the ring of an illness, but was a proudly self-attributed name for people who thought of themselves as highly effective. It was no longer an affliction of proletarians, but only of exterminating angels. How could it have been otherwise? Computer interfaces, electronic messaging systems, and digital networks couldn't transmit the juices of piss, sperm, and shit. They left incarnation behind in the emergency lane of their freeways. The information society *skeeze* can only take the most gossamer part of his being with him. Words, images, sounds. Sometimes a small rollaway. A strict trav-eller's minimum, in other words. Fat leather suitcases, hatboxes, wardrobes and the rest of the luggage associ-ated with long vacations somewhat paradoxically remained the paraphernalia of porters and the assembly lines of heavy industry, manufacturing, and machine tools. Useless anachronisms obsoleted by the new econ-omy and discredited by the new modernity. In fact, what people were now after was a *permanent* vacation. No longer a temporary parentheses, but a lifeline etched across a silicon palm.

I, Skeeze!

The happy *skeeze* was the love child of the liquid dreams of the counterculture and the credo of the new entrepreneurs. Just dip into the literature of the period and you'll see it. Jeremy Rifkin, the activist-prophet of avant-garde capitalism, announced the emergence of a new type of human being. While I don't particularly care for this kind of prophecy, I have to admit that to a cer-tain degree I recognized myself in it. I, a *skeeze*! "People of the twenty-first century are as likely to perceive them-selves as nodes on embedded networks of shared interests as they are to perceive themselves as autonomous agents in a Darwinian world of competitive survival. For them, personal freedom will be about the right to be included in webs of mutual relationships . . . they will be part of the first generation of the age of access."[64] Rifkin's book hit the shelves at exactly the right moment, just as the internet bubble was at its most bloated. I was leaving a performance piece in Paris called *Gravity 0* where I had watched artificial snowflakes fall on the naked body of actress Mallaury Nataf.[65] "Today," Rifkin goes on, "the idea of measuring the value of computers according to their weight would be regarded as completely crazy, especially when it is known that a greetings card equipped with a chip contains more data-processing power than there was on the whole planet in 1945."[66] Leaving the exposition, I jotted this down in a little notebook: "Idiotic fantasy. Lousy execution. *Gravity 0* is aptly named 0." The judgment was a little unfair. After all, it was a salutary to the degree that it was an attempt to represent the thing: weightless mankind.

> The age of access is bringing with it a new type of human being. Completely at ease in cyberspace, where they pass a significant part of their life . . . they are used to free software . . . indeed . . . they live in a world of seven second spots, are accustomed to having near-instantaneous access to all kinds of information [certainly], do not have very long attention spans and are represented as more spontaneous and less deliberate than the preceding generations [obvious, but after all, Rifkin must be pushing 60]. They conceive their professional activity as a form of play and prefer being perceived as creators more than as good workers [I can confirm this]. They have grown up in a 'just-in-time' work world and are accustomed to temp jobs [definitely]. Their language is made up of images rather than words [is it still?]. They spend as much time in the company of fictional characters as with other individuals [indeed].[67]

Rifkin's prophecy brought together all of the truisms of virtuality. It sounded a lot like the kind of diatribe foisted on you by a cab driver, when you had only expected on getting a ride: "Well! You know, kids these days no longer make any distinction between their stupid videogames and the real world. No surprise that they don't show any respect for anything any more." What a disgusted Flaubert called "received ideas." However, to be fair to Rifkin, I had to admit that both he and the taxi driver were right about one thing: since the letters *www* had been added to the dictionary of behavior, it was clear that our relationship to the world had changed.

Like the other skeezes, I spent a lot of time boosting, the kind of pontification on hot topics that makes you popular among media people. Boosting basically means delivering a series of pitches, the pitch being an oratory exercise that consists in presenting a hot concept of the moment in order to make money, whether it's to sell merchandise, an ad campaign, a TV show, an art exhibition or a corporate project. The important thing about pitching is to be neither too ahead of one's times or too far behind them. Too advanced and no one will get it. Too old school and you're finished. In each case, the concept will be rejected. "Every pitch has its moment" is rule number one for the pitcher. To grasp this principle, you have to understand that a concept is sellable not because it is accurate, but because it is talked up in the right way at the right time. Which brings us to rule number two: "the pitch is adjustable." The pitcher has to adapt the style and timing of the pitch to his audience. There are *esoteric pitches,* directed at refined connoisseurs and which must be delivered in a way that makes them as opaque as possible so that the mark becomes convinced of the visionary character of the idea. The art here is to evoke a sense of mystery and initiation. A dash of poetry can be most useful here. On the other hand, the *didactic pitch* is the opposite kind of animal, designed for use with the clueless. For example, you have a meeting with a venture capitalist interested in investing in a start-up based on something young people are doing. Here, the presentation needs to be clear, didactic, and concise. Obviously, there are potentially an infinite number of pitches that a pitcher can deploy, according to his specific sensibility, vocabulary, and style. Worth mentioning is the *teaser pitch*, which gets going with a little anecdote that whets the curiosity of the pitchee. Then there's the speed pitch, or *elevator speech*, designed to persuade one's interlocutor in the time it takes to move between the 3rd and 34th floors of a skyscraper. The *physical pitch* employs sex-appeal to close the deal, while the user of the *shy pitch* adopts a studied timidity. Finally, well-known individuals whose inner simplicity has proven immune to the perverting influence of fame have recourse to the *humble pitch*.

Towards the middle of the 90s, the vast majority of pitches surfed on the tides of the fluid fantasy. I jumped on the bandwagon, pitching the concept of *transversality*. I said: Look at all those shops with half a dozen different things going on in them! Combination bar-thrift stores, art-galleries-cum-shoe-stores, cafés offering Thai massage, night clubs with workout programs—the old categories of being and having have passed away. Thanks to the power of the URL, borders are vanishing and we are being transformed not only into masters and owners of nature, but also into to controllers of the air, masters of times and space. We are now *simultaneously* artists, musicians, DJs, directors, producers, advertisers, and business actors. I gathered arguments from all over the place to prove that yes, the human body was henceforth an unstable and temporary platform, living halfway between the real and the virtual in a temporality of varying velocities, where the immediate shaded into the slow without ever clocking a moment of rest. As for biology, life is information. Only information is capable of resisting entropy. Thus, information flows are the principle of life, and those who would seek to oppose them are the agents of death. As for physics: matter does not exist—matter is only crystallized information, unstable, condemned to a disequilibrium without end. It follows that we too are equally unstable. Physics again: space does not exist. There's only crystallized time, and it seeks only to dissolve us. I dreamt of being rootless, wandering with nothing left to lose, a vagabond, a stranger. The world wide web opened the way for us, showed us the great road of phony wandering, allowed us to become anonymous simulacra floating among the virtual cosmos. It was the ideal world for the body without organs. The ascetic I had formerly admired, the unnamable that I had explored abandoned their missions in the blink of an eye. Being-against had morphed into being-for. For the unstable, for transformation, hybridization and metamultiplication of identities. For the flux, for the networks, for a temporality wholly contracted into real-time. For TRANSVERSALITY. This treason of the flesh: I confess that I too, succumbed.

Soap Bubble

Cyberpunk was an early vehicle for the contemporary hatred of the flesh and techno-idolatry. *Anti-Œdipus* had led small-minded intellectuals to hail the coming of the Flux-man. I came on the scene at third phase of the gathering wave. How did the mythology of the Night pave the way for the triumph of the networks? This mendacious mythology in which nobodies could pretend that they were demigods? Psychedelic night of chemical mis-adventure, where between one creature and another, a thousand lies are confessed as if they were deep truths. Artificial night of the 80s, when transvestitism became more real than reality. This night is now readily available in broad daylight, available in heart of capitalism itself, everywhere in the districts and precincts of the infosphere. The *simulacrum* was not denounced. Baudrillard might go on thundering against the false as much as he liked. His ideas wilted, died, and were buried. Artists celebrated their new territory, a mixture of the digital, of cybernetic dreams, virtual reality, and multiple personalities. There was no longer much to thunder against. It was time to have fun. It was in this spirit, and with the beautiful lucidity of one who feels himself touched on the shoulder by death that Gilles Châtelet, the mathematician, teacher, philosopher, and kindred soul looked back over the faded photos of the nights of his thirties. His language felt a little outdated, but it made little difference—everything was already there. Everything, at the dawn of the 80s, a November Sunday in 1979, to be exact. The date of the "Red and Gold" night at the Paris nightclub the *Palace*. The body cedes its place to the horizontal notion that power is a function of networks. "Those who didn't experience the end of the 70s will never know the sweetness of life in those times, the deliciousness like the trembling slipper, the *escarpolette* in Fragonard's painting[68] where History swings between an *Ancien Régime* and the stir of a revolution. To many here tonight, Paris, Europe, the entire planet seemed a light as a soap bubble—the spirit of the Night knew that the master is not really he who possesses, but he who can unleash, the guardian of the flames of thresholds, the pivot on which a thousand action turn." Gilles Châtelet knew that the revolution in the making was that of the Free-Marketers, of Thatcher, Reagan, and the conservatives. What he didn't know was that their posterity was guaranteed. Already, the sweat of dancers was mixing with the information flows. One of the things about nightlife was that it didn't matter how much property you owned, as far as access was concerned. But at the super-exclusive *Palace*, it was like Rifkin and Gibson *avant la lettre*. It was a place where the underground was transformed into a springboard to VIP status. The magic kingdom of deviant bodies, of hybrids and trans- was getting ready for the digital age. It was like a kind of Web-Tuesday that still had a party atmosphere. Not for long. The night lived out its last days at the Palace, people said. In the 90s, no one celebrated anything anymore. One *upgraded* oneself hierarchically. One sought placement opportunities. What had once been the mission of *Palace* impresario Fabrice, prince of the night, to "have the worlds of money, fashion and intellectuals collide, to make that collision *swing*, and then to make it so that the most daring nobodies could come and add their spice to the soup of great somebodies,"[69] now was an everyday exercise. The bodies were ready to reap the wages of their betrayal. Everything was in place. The cyberpunks, the flux-bodies, the networks of the night. Only capitalism was missing from the feast, and capitalism's revolution, which was to be fought by the inheritors of the revolt of the 60s, waited impatiently for master to arrive.

At the end of the 90s even the newspapers were rooting for this obsession with mankind's fluid destiny. I read that IBM was gradually getting rid of its offices in favor of a mobile labor force made up of free-roaming, high-connectivity workers. This was called *hosting*: employees no longer had permanent offices, but instead, would book time in banks of office space whose location depended on where they were at any given moment. According to a study by the *Harvard Business Review*, a combination of *hosting*, closing underused office space, and relocating certain centers in lower-cost sites saved IBM 1.4 billion in location costs. I also read about the gradual elimination of warehouse stocks. A dinosaur of the old economy like General Electric had closed 26 of its 34 warehouses in the U.S. and replaced 20 consumer service centers with a single central client services unit.[70] The major record companies were announcing the death of physical music media, which was on the verge of being replaced by online distribution systems. In the view of the consulting company Marketing Tracking International (MTI), by 2020 more than 20% of worldwide music sales would be made through online distribution channels. To explain why the economy was suddenly becoming weightless, the groupthink of the times latched onto an old maxim from the dawn of the information age: Moore's Law. According to Moore's Law, the processing power of computers roughly doubles each year.[71] In his book *One Market Under God*, Thomas Frank, one of the most refined observers of the U.S. economy, minutely described the dreams, even hallucinations, inspired by Moore's Law. "From the rousing op-eds of *Wired* and

Forbes, from CEO conference calls, from the bubbling announcements on CNBC, from the ecstatic Babel of motivational seminars, came word of the miraculous advance: through feats of sheer positive thinking, Business Man had overturned the principles of accounting, had smashed the barriers of price-to-earnings, had redrawn the map of competition, had thrown off the dead hand of the physical world! The country's gross national product, we exulted, weighed less than ever before! We dealt in ideas rather than things! And just as the laws of Newton had given way to those of the microchip, so scarcity itself, the curse of the material world, had been overcome once and for all. Not even the Fed could call the New Economy back to earth."[72]

All over again, Moore's Law ordained that the spirit should have a single destiny. It halted it, froze it, bound it—*clack!*—a lock snapped shut. And so we moved from one prison to another. From the confinement of despair to the constraints of the fluid. The mechanism of treason remained as Julien Benda had defined it: the mind invents laws to explain change, then it forgets that it invented them. It thus leaves itself no choice but to submit. In Benda's times, the law in question was dialectical materialism. It showed that the History pointed towards the East, to the dictatorship of the proletariat, to the abolition of social classes. In doing so, it manufactured a kind of inexorability, an *inevitable* destiny. Now it was Moore's Law that one pointed to everywhere as the new cipher of man's future.[73] For a long time, I meditated on this irresistible need of men to believe in the empirical laws they devise. Does the law create destiny, or does destiny create the law? Error, plus faith in error is a force of awesome power. Doubtless they speed up the destiny that they cause us to believe in, they hurl us into it, for better or for worse. The speculative bubble and dictatorship thus have the same origins: what is no more than a streak of bad bets gets itself accepted as the as the only truth. The bubble and dictatorship don't have the same human consequences, you'll tell me. But look at the consequences, both for the spirit and the flesh.

The manias that overtake a given epoch force you to believe along with them. They come at you with their committed, their imbecilic YES. They compel you to build your life around the things that are going on. They grab you and set you down on the rails of a shared reality—a reality in fact built of invented laws. Are the laws invented out of cunning, or out of optimism? There's some calculation there, of course, there are interests at stake. But the novelty of the new reality wins you over. Because it's a change of pace, it's more fun. Also because you can make money off novelty. And so the presses start up, spewing out a simple faith for simple people. Before dialectical materialism got a bad name, the law trended more or less to the left. But from the moment it was replaced by the law of the fluid, the compass spun to the right. In each case, one was told that paradise was just around the corner. Governments really change very little. Only the laws of becoming change, and when they are changed, they affect the lives of everyone, regardless of whether they made the laws or not. "If you ask me, the motives of the people who brandish this method are obvious," wrote Benda, "they are the motives of attackers who tell the peoples of the world: our actions are justified because they are dictated by destiny. Adopt them. Adopt destiny."[74] An adoption. The word was well-chosen, for the rebel body had changed its identity too.

The treason of the flesh left us no choice. We could either be voluntary nomads, happy *skeezes*, in other words, people of the great liquefaction, or else we would suffer the fate of involuntary nomads, forced to follow the currents of capital against their conscience. It would be wrong to say that *all* of the intellegentsia had jumped on board, leaving *all* of society behind it. A few intellectuals remained back on the docks. Pierre Bourdieu, for example. He did not take part in the betrayal. I watched him hang out alongside the picketing railroad workers during the huge 1995 strike in France. I saw him again, haunting the narrow rue de Dragon the following year, defending a few hundred homeless from an eviction notice. Obviously, the great liquefaction had its refusniks. They spoke of the ravages of neoliberalism, the scandal of social exclusion, the dictatorship of the market. In the spirit of maintaining a minimal level of debate they were allowed to speak at the margins. They were listened to indulgently, with a bit of pity, as one listens to maladapted children.[75]

One must understand that with the triumph of the fluid body, even the idea that there existed *some thing* like a social body with a length, a width, a depth and rights appeared farfetched. I was thus pleased to learn that some intellectuals persisted in recalling that before becoming a cyborg, the connected human being was the basic unit of a community of mouths, flesh and egos to feed. Nevertheless, there was always this perceptible air of laziness, of a lack of imagination, of a discussion that went in the right direction but that used the wrong language. There was a sense of nostalgia for a time when the sides were well-defined and responsibility clear. For the times when art still had a history. An enormous gulf separated the two generations of rebels. These were two generations whose aesthetics and politics lay light-years apart. In them, I saw how the intellect becomes rigid when it stops looking for territory outside its own memories. They could not accept the dissolution of the old powers, power's new invisibility, its fluidity. They were hurt by the disdain of the *skeezes*. So they tried to recreate the frame of reference of their childhood: a territory occupied by a nation that delegates sovereignty to representatives according to democratic principles, and with, on this territory, private persons who exchange goods and services according to contractual rules defined and controlled by the State. In the name of this framework, they rejected complexity and condemned the networks of transnational power, which always had to be "hidden." They deplored that space was no longer governed except by immaterial and "irrational" capital flows. Yet they could only respond to modernity in a reactionary way. How could it have been any different? They had witnessed the career of the welfare state across a half-century. It had worked out okay, after all. It had sought to reduce the gap between the rich and the poor. Courageously, it had sought to counterbalance private interests with public services. It had accomplished all that at the cost of a certain excitement, it is true. Creature comforts were boring. Social democracy was boring. Reformism was boring. The middle classes, public amenities, growth, electric blenders, mopeds, all this was pretty boring. Progress, boring. The national budget, boring, the course of history, boring, hierarchy, organization, five year plans: boring. Boring like tortoiseshell sunglasses and velour jackets. Boring like tobacco pipes, like socialism. Boring like veterans' cere-monies, like sexually-segregated dormitories, like cur-fews. Yet beyond the great cultural transformations of the 70s, from which resulted an even greater sense of ennui, the ennui driving the nostalgia for pot, for any-thing retro, for the return of funk, for the idolatry of the victims of rock and roll, or for the rock and roll the charts forgot—beyond all this, the welfare state still pret-ty much *did its job*.

But it was hard to be satisfied with that. We had to come up with something new. Neither this old-fangled reaction engine nor the more modern collusion between partying and cyberspace. Not nostalgia for the old world of territory. Not the *skeezes* of the infosphere. What we needed was a dissident strategy adapted to the information age but one that would be neither cynical nor reactionary. Something that would make use of speed to promote slowness, something disembodied to reclaim the right to incarnation, something mobile and liquid that would fight in the name of solidity, some-thing virtual with a real conscience. That, I believe, was the task of our 90s. A sustained battle to reinvent revolt in a form that would be neither a quest for cool nor a reactionary retreat.

THE NEW INCARNATION
What is invisible, but lies in plain sight?

"*One feels that these awful wretches dreamt of an altogether different world, of a beyond that would never become a 'here,' of a world that would never seize up to become ordinary and banal . . . that would forever preserve within its heart the fire out of which it was born. Men raging against the Destiny that held them fast and ground them down, these men were prepared to gamble, and what matter if the upshot could only be death, death in a condition of absolute freedom, consequent on the unrestrained expansion of their desire . . .*"[76]

"*One dead, 180 wounded, a* carabinieri *and a young woman seriously—this is the outcome of the confrontations between the Italian police and the antiglobalism demonstrators, Friday July 20th in Genoa.*"[77]

It was clear to the suffocating man that capital was getting out of control. Each morning, he would get threatening mail from the Gene Police. The climbing rosebush he had given himself for his birthday was a copyrighted genetically-engineered product. He was not permitted to duplicate it, breed it, or distribute its genetic code, the accompanying papers told him, via any existing or future media. It was only a warning notice, but still . . . One evening as he arrived at his apartment, he saw that he had mail waiting for him. Freetime, a European subsidiary of Disney, was announcing the privatization of his street. He would have fought it, but it was already a done deal. He found the co-op meetings intolerably boring, and so the deal between the company and the residents of the street was pitched and closed without his even being aware of it. Security, community, and tranquility were the three bases of the project. The bar where he used to go to tuck into a dry martini at the end of the day was slated to be replaced by a fitness center. Access to the street would be protected by a gate with a digicode and surveillance cameras.

The Gene Police and Freetime, Inc. weren't the only ones laying siege to his mailboxes. Each day, his postal and electronic mailboxes alike were subject to an inexhaustible stream of junk mail. The suffocating man had mixed feelings about this. The barrage of communication made him a little less alone. Lots of businesses knew his name and his address. They were always giving him gifts or special offers. That said, he wasn't a complete idiot. It was clear to him that businesses were gradually encroaching on his property. All he had to do was look through his mail. The number of coupons was diminishing, while the subscription offers increased. Freetime even proposed a deal whereby he would agree to cede ownership of his apartment in exchange for unlimited access to the company's services: vacations, fitness programs, sport club memberships, amusement parks, cable TV channels, magazine subscriptions, and so on. Should he resign himself to these changes, the suffocating man asked himself? It was a fact of life that the extension of the sphere of capital would reduce his autonomy, but should he really put up with the privatization of his rosebush and his street? This was in any case was the question for those living in the New Architecture of the United World.

Unexpected forms of resistance materialized to counter this new embrace of capital. Peasants rallied against the privatization of grain species, the slothful struggled against the privatization of time, digital pirates demonstrated against the privatization of networks, while indigenous cultures rebelled against the sale of their genetic traits to the laboratories of Big Science. Should he call for them to band together? He could not keep from thinking of the NAUW's damned invisible barriers. The endings of the scenes he was watching play out had been rigged. The scenes had really already been played out.

Moreover, it was clear to him that the nature of these rebellions had changed. They were less ideological than when he was young, less arrogant, less hierarchic, more disorganized, more fragmented, and also more fragile. They wobbled. The word "revolution" was never uttered. Oversight was preferred to taking over. The theme of the day was reconquest, not conquest. Finally, much to his taste, the new rebels did not care for leaders.

"In the end, everything is connected," the suffocating man said to himself. "My rosebush, Freetime, coded entries. Capitalism has crossed the line. I thought it had to stop sometime, but no, it just keeps on going." A few

days later, he made contact with a group of hackers in order to launch a vast parasite attack on cyberspace to slow the flows of information. He slipped on a harness and chained himself to the tollbooth of a large freeway as an example. It was a ridiculous gesture, but it took guts all the same. When the patrolmen finally succeeded in dislodging him, the last words he uttered before disappearing into the back of the police wagon were, "I am heavy, I've got mass, and I am MODERN."

We have crossed the laughing desert of *mass dandyism*. We have bathed in the liquid of the *skeezes*. To keep them at our back, we had to reinvent a way to go on, to continue existing. This struggle took the form of a campaign of war. Not the kind of war in which one waves flags. No! A war where the body struggles with the mind, where they twist and writhe without knowing who or what to start with. It is not easy to fight against laughter, against cynicism, against resignation and despair. It is not easy to stand up for the good old dimension of time and space against the noise of an epoch clamoring for the liquidation of everything. In contrast to the generations that came before us, we did not base our demands on theory. We acted out of intuition, and without completely shunting aside the beautiful chaos that we had learned to make our home in. We were not after power. All we wanted was to be left alone. Yes! All we wanted was the right to bow out of the game. But even that was refused us.

The episodes of this war coincided with the story of my adolescence. It's a drama in four acts. Each of them is a moment in the mind and body's hunt for a strategy of rebellion to escape the captivity and break the stranglehold of the times. The first act tells of the opening we made in the closed world of the end of history by calling for a *temporary exterior*. Act II shows how poetic language reappeared to confront the cold language of the last men. In Act III we see how by remaking the body flesh and masking our faces we attempted to banish the image and block the flows. The last act recounts the birth of an open-ended dialectic and a nomad resistance that can bring back human will as a force of History.

Because I'm not very big on cliffhangers, I want to give away the ending right now. It's not a Hollywood ending. All we've done is sow a seed in the middle of the mud. What sort of creature will bloom there? No one knows. Apart from the theater of it all, nothing has changed. The mainstream has seen and heard nothing. Once again, it has proved Flaubert right: everything changes, but the imbecile heart of man endures. The silent majorities still vote and the triumph of the flows continues unabated. They vote for pigs that despise them and condescend to them. Television lulls them to sleep in making them believe that seeing is the same as acting. They slump in their chairs, grow soft, and forget themselves. Governments whose only legitimacy lies in the silence of the silent majorities bring their auctions of the public welfare to a close. Business leaders put the finishing touches on their penal colonies by adding the language of social justice to their projects, giving them environmentally-conscious veneers, even tricking them out as goodwill missions.

So much for the mud. Now for the seeds. In the hall where the play was played, the spectators were delirious. Rather than ending up concocting a pleasing apology for the economy, they finished by skewering the spirit of the times on the end of a rapier. It's no longer the season for resignation. The laughter is dying down. Cynicism is already dead. The producers of the play don't see it yet (since they are banking on stupidity) but that's how it is—cynicism is indeed dead. Or rather, it is dying. It's roots are sunk deep into the innermost strata of our times. Many healthy vines likely remain, but it is a dying plant. Slowly, we are emerging from its age of darkness. We are leaving behind us the *spirit of endings* that was its great flower, and a little groggily, we are entering an age of willful frankness, of an innocence both considered and wise. It's the reopening of the world after closure for renovations—and maybe it would be appropriate to announce it the way department stores do. Goodbye dandyism. Goodbye *skeezes*. Not there is no one left to laugh at us and we can say: we are *lucid romantics*.

Romanticism is a curious beast. Each time you try to close your hand around it, it will slip through your fingers. It will flash up on your left, suddenly materialize on your right, pop up where you never expected to see it. Romanticism is not white like snow. Some even say that it has blood on its hands. So imagine just for a second a line outside the door to a courtroom. At the end of the line, there's a judge presiding. In line, not people, but BAD WORDS, shooting words, in fact . . . name please? Communism. Occupation? Collective ownership of the means of production, abolition of social classes. Number killed? More than 10 million. Next! Name? National Socialism. Occupation? Extermination of the Jews, affirmation of the superiority of the Aryan Race. Number killed? More than 10 million. Next! Name? Capitalism. Occupation? Private ownership of the means of production, accumulation of capital. Number killed? Still counting. Wait here, and send the next one in. Name? Romanticism. Occupation? Literature. Number killed? Never could say . . .

Romance can go ahead and add an important-sounding –*ism* to itself if it likes, it still won't get into the museum of deadly ideologies. That said, it can't be denied that romanticism had a hand in the barbarisms enumerated above. You can see its dim silhouette in the background of each group photo. Romanticism is that desire of the heart in whose name one will tear oneself apart, in whose name one will fight, in whose name one will torture. Only this:

you never follow the trail all the way back to the soul. Instead it's the hand dealing the blows that is guilty. There's no doubt that romanticism played a role in stirring up the people of Europe. We don't deny the fact that it made tongues wag, territories mobilize, and blood stir to the point of transforming culture into a war machine. Initially, when it emerged at the end of the 18th century, romanticism was poetic. It played the tumultuous music of sentiment against the icy Reason of the Enlightenment. No harm in that. Only this: In 1789, the ideas of the Enlightenment became incarnate in a Nation. France. The King's head fell from his shoulders. The soldiers of the Year II massed. We heard the name Bonaparte, then Napoleon. We conquered and we pillaged in the name of Reason. Meanwhile, romanticism was enlisted to defend Germany. French Genius, German Genius: pick your side. This is how one can argue that romanticism fed the roots of all our European nationalisms and their inventory of murders. The same could be said of revolutionary lyricism, that insurgent romanticism, that red, proletarian romanticism born out of the ashes of the French revolution and nourished to consummation by utopian socialist writings until it sprang forth fully-grown in the Commune and swept across Europe all the way to Russia, where it froze and hardened before going on to conquer China only to burst forth once again, even more passionately, in Latin America, in Japan, in Italy, in France, under the name of the radical left.

So why, why after listening to this litany of accusations, why would anyone be excited to see a resurgence of *lucid romanticism*? What could be so different about *this* romanticism that it would not end up engendering new tragedies in its turn? Why is it that as time has passed, romanticism has dwindled into a kind of storage shed into which one habitually throws sappy poems, maudlin short stories, throwaway sentimentalities, tear-jerker movies, and mass-market bodice-rippers? Sometimes they even toss living things in there. Utopians, gentle dreamers, a spritz of idealists, a handful of teenagers who still believe that hands are for petting rather than for fist fucking. And so this is why I throw open the doors of the shed without fear, intent on dissecting the beast. I don't have to worry about ending up like Pandora. Out of the many bygone romanticisms, we have chosen the best and left the worst. We have held on to the aesthetic of the will. We added irony and doubt. We kept alive the idea that man was capable of acting upon History, but we abandoned the grotesque heroism of the avant-gardes that imagined they could overturn it. We rediscovered the earth, the poetry and the blood with which bodies embody themselves, but we rejected the land and the idea of a nation determined by the idea of the State. We dusted off the dialectic by opening up its horizon of possibility. Resistance's borderless nomadism was our creed, and we fought the happy *skeeze* of global hip.

Lucid romanticism couldn't even hurt a fly. Because it doesn't truly believe. It only wants to believe. This is why it is constantly apologizing for its outbursts. If I had to describe it as a style of writing, I'd say that it's a succession of short sentences. One word then another. Terse adjectives. Then suddenly, a long phrase gesturing reluctantly towards the infinite. It had been so long since we had dared to reach out that we had almost forgotten how to do it. Matter-of-fact lowdowns, snide analyses, we could spin those out in our sleep, but what about visions? Flights? No, no, those only led to crashes. But couldn't you try a more guarded lyricism? Not possible, that only led to mockery. Our most rapt passages will always be soiled by a hint of doubt.

Our romanticism is like a survivor of a disastrous ship-wreck. We faced the tides of resignation and stupidity and did not go under. This shipwreck has made us carriers of a time against the times. Our ideal? It is farfetched and shaky. Our determination? It has had its legs cut off, but it is still breathing. Given such limitations, what kind of rebellion are we still capable of? A rebellion intoxicated with style, but without greed. Ascetic as regards consumption, but hedonist and embodied in its response to the world. This sort of style, I'd like to think, is characterized by a constant insurrection, a revolution every minute that aims not at shortening the interval between desire and satisfaction, but rather at increasing it in order to desire that much more. I believe in that peculiar rebellion of "I"s, that movement *inside* consciousness that the Greeks called harmony. I believe that there is a crossroads where the desire for reserve flows into the great reserve of desire. The I of the anxious mind that questions and weighs and doubts without coming to rest. The I of Artaud, stifled by the flesh. The I that refuses to be bowed by the nonchalance of *mass dandyism*, and finally, the Mediterranean "I" of the summer of Camus, who not so long ago made such an happy marriage of the body of pleasure and the body of justice on a beach in Oran. It is high time we reread Camus.

"Only slowly, and with great difficulty does the writer surpass the romantic that he once was, and that refuses to die," writes literary critic René Girard.[78] Girard thought that the writer had to avoid the snares of pride and recognize that from his earliest childhood he will be as motivated by jealousy, vanity and impotent hatred as the snob is. The snob of our times is a happy *skeeze*, a nomadic hipster for whom there are no longer any boundaries between the worlds of capital, art, and communication. *Lucid romanticism* transports us from this state and restores the sense of childhood after the I has made its long wanderings through the jealousies, vanities, and impotent rages of adolescense. In contrast to Girard's romantics, we're neither part of the big lie nor on the side of truth. Instead, we're balancing on the stretching tightrope of lost illusions. And we will not give up.

A Marvelous Telegram

Act I. We have created an "elsewhere" in the closed world of the end of history. Faced with the dismal nadir of market democracy, we had to respond quickly. We had to invent a temporary alternative, a *provisional outside* to the New Architecture of the United World's all-encompassing logic. In one fell swoop, we tossed the theses of *definitive* liberation in the laundry hamper. The washing machine spun round and round endlessly, until one day we discovered a text published in 1990 by a tiny publishing house in Williamsburg, Brooklyn, a book signed by a certain Mr. Hakim Bey.[79] Its title was an acronym made up of three letters: "TAZ," for "Temporary Autonomous Zone." At the time no one would have been able to imagine how, by a chain of magical echoes, the sound of these words would come to irradiate the scenes of our adolescence. From the ravers to the eco-warriors, from Australia to England. Mr. Bey argued that the TAZ was the opposite of a political dogma. It was a fleeting concept: "I have deliberately refrained from defining the

111

TAZ—I circle around the subject, firing off exploratory beams."[80] Further on, he described it as "an uprising which does not engage directly with the State, a guerilla operation which liberates an area (of land, of time, of imagination) and then dissolves itself to re-form elsewhere/elsewhen, before the State can crush it." Bey's rants drew from occultism, from martial arts, and from science fiction. He was actually indebted to Sci-Fi for the whole concept—specifically, Bruce Sterling's *Islands in the Net*—as he admitted towards the beginning of TAZ, Sterling's story being based on "the assumption that the decay of political systems will lead to a decentralized proliferation of experiments in living: giant worker-owned corporations, independent enclaves devoted to "data piracy," Green-Social-Democrat enclaves, Zerowork enclaves, anarchist liberated zones, etc."[81]

The concept of the TAZ arrived just in time, just a few weeks after the end of history. It had the sweet lilt of those expressions that are incapable of liberating bodies but nevertheless allow the spirit breathing room. *Temporary Autonomous Zone*. Stop. To be content with an unstable state of hope. Stop. In the time of the confinement, to think of a beyond not as a place, but as a moment in time. Stop. To never more exhaust one's forces against capitalism. Stop. To prefer the dodge, the back roads, the banquets among friends. Stop. Not to seek to abolish power. Stop. To not give a fuck. Stop. To enjoy the enclaves and to get one's enjoyment through the enclaves. Stop. To view small, ordinary things done with grace as acts of resistance. Stop. Liberation is a vain word. Stop. The TAZ is a vacant lot, a single night. Stop. A woman's handbag hanging slightly open. Stop. Two lovers who whisper to each other and fuck. The fingers of the watchmaker on a pocket-watch at a neighborhood movie theater. Stop. Knowing that everything that has not yet been withered by the state and the market will end up being withered by the state and the market. Stop. Meanwhile, the TAZ is possible. Stop. Creation cannot be repeated, it is a TAZ. Production repeats itself, it's boring. The TAZ is a gap in time that has no other referents beyond itself. An uncommercial orgasm, an uncommercial exchange, uncommercial music, uncommercial images. Stop. The gratuity of mouth-to mouth, word-of-mouth, ankle chains, the erogenous free trade zone between two bodies. Stop. The TAZ is a breath of fresh air, a marvelous telegram.

> Here we are crawling the cracks between walls of church state school and factory, all the paranoid monoliths. Cut off from the tribe by feral nostalgia we tunnel after lost words, imaginary bombs.[82]

The TAZ couldn't let us down, because it promised nothing. Nothing, in any case, beyond a disposable autonomy, perpetually renewed through experiences of celebration or resistance. Amidst the wreckage of dead ideas, it served a certain purpose, gave us a purchase, like when you suddenly get a grip on a stripped screw that wouldn't turn. To put it briefly, it turned depressive readings of History on their head. In the face of failed revolutions, it celebrated the evanescence of insurrection. "*Surgo*—rise up, surge. *Insurgo*—rise up, raise oneself up. A bootstrap operation. A *CYA* to that wretched parody of the karmic circle, the futility of historical revolutions. The slogan 'Revolution!' has mutated from tocsin to toxin, a malign pseudo-Gnostic fate-trap . . ."[83] Through the TAZ, the most insignificant acts might suddenly reveal within them the seeds of a cathedral. These TAZ were built by the traveling caravans of ravers, by the first followers of Spiral Tribe, crossing Europe loaded with sounds of inner laceration, why not also by compulsive stamp collectors, by crackheads in their crackhouses . . . Build them everywhere! The TAZ gave meaning to our negations. Hope against a backdrop of finitude. Ideals against a backdrop of nihilism. Purity against a backdrop of despair.

Let us not forget, everything we did was simultaneously *de-crypted* by a throng of imbecilic pundits. The imbeciles went on about, for example, how we were organized into tribes—these are the rastas, these are the goths, these are the ravers, these are the hip-hops, these are the technos, etc.—and how each tribe had its own codes and values differentiating it from the others. They told us how tribalism could be understood as a consumerist holism. They told us how it would eat away at the social fabric, that it was based on regressive and narcissistic behavior, how it represented the progress of materialism and loss of all moral reference points. That it was linked to the crisis of institutions and authority. Finally, that the disaffection for politics it represented was wedded to a retreat back into the self. Whatever. It's true we started out with a hatred of politics. We hated it with an intensity the men and women of the 70s will never understand. We hated it because we saw that it was devoid of lyricism, devoid of dreams, devoid of ambition, devoid of style. It was nothing more than a party for exhausted has-beens. Thanks to the TAZ, we were able to reinvent and rediscover everything.

At this time, I was living in London and divided my time between the Jamaican neighborhood of Ladbroke Grove, doing some *fin-de-siècle* posing, and pursuing a retro passion for Mongol rock. In short, I was quite the postmodern young fellow, and postmodern was a word I used at the slightest provocation, alternating it with the word *chaos*, which in this context, meant more or less the same thing. These were the days when ecstasy was streaming up from Ibiza and pouring its artificial sunshine out on the abandoned factories of northern England. Syncretism was the latest thing. The yuppies from South Ken had shamelessly adopted a lifestyle mixing Zen exercise, dark beer, blond women, sushi combos, and swinging. Almost as soon as I got off the ferry, I learned that "something was happening" over on Claremont Road. The Transportation Minister had announced the construction of a freeway linking Wanstead and East London. An entire neighborhood as well as one of the oldest forests in Greater London was threatened by the project and the opposition of the locals had failed to stop it.

When I got there, on a cold and rainy evening, I was greeted by walled-up windows and scattered wind-splayed streetlamps. Motionless bulldozers sat heavily in the darkness, reminiscent of looming dinosaur skeletons in a natural history museum. In this place lived a baroque colony of ravers, artists, ecologists, and lost souls, all brought together by the fight against the construction of the M11. The buildings were linked by strange basement passages and in front of them, rusted out car hulks served as flower boxes. Wanting to appear clever, I hazarded this grand pronouncement: "The squats are just like Ibis Hotels, only in the squats, you have rust-stained concrete floors instead of fake marble and crushed beer cans instead of minibars." But I had got it wrong. Claremont Road was not a scene for the snide. At the entrance to the construction site, in the middle of the bulldozers, in this atmosphere of pre-demolition, the look on people's faces told me: "Stop where you are, young man! Take off your mask, put away your phony snobbery, your fake ridicule. You can keep your dimples, but we're not interested in the rest of it." I stayed there five months.

The battle between Claremont Road and the M11 lasted until November 1994. The district was finally demolished, and the strip of freeway was soon jammed with big black taxis. However, an entire generation of English activists found new inspiration there. John Jordan was one of them. An art teacher and an artist, he had been at the center of the fierce eco-warrior campaigns of the second half of the 90s. I ran into him several years later, after the Seattle demonstrations, after the media phenomenon of antiglobalization, after the unfurling of the whole circus that makes one forget where and when the first tremors occurred. John did not remember me from Claremont Road. After all, I was just a baby then. But nostalgia wasn't what we were there for. I asked him if others at the battle of Claremont Road had thought of it as a TAZ. For it was a situation exactly resembling the ones Bey described: a temporary zone where a joyous chaos reigned, transformed by the grace of art into a community of resistance. "Maybe, maybe not," John answered. He lent me a book by George McKay called *DIY Culture*, an anthology about the counterculture in England. One of the pieces in the book, "The Art of Necessity" told the story of Claremont Road.[84]

The power of impermanence! Here was the first condition of *lucid romanticism*, a diptych uniting the acceptance of fate and the rejection of resignation: "We always knew that one day all of this would be rubble . . ." We could not believe in the reality of our goal. We had to learn to seize the moment. Since the birth of a modern understanding of History, the people of the West have always had a project: the spreading of Enlightenment as a project, technological progress as a project, the Hegelian dialectic and the rise of the bourgeois liberal state as a project, the classless society as a project, the society of nations and perpetual peace as a project, environmentalism, feminism, hallucinogens, communes, liberation . . . in contrast to such programmatic ambitions, we needed to learn to be. Deprived of history, we needed to learn to act. Without any other perspective beyond a pile of stones, to learn to love.

Like the *temporary* in TAZ, the power of *impermanence* qualified every action done in its name with a skepticism as to the long-term effects of action. At the heart of rebellion lay the conviction that rebellion's agenda was unattainable. Both ideas shared a basic pessimism, but each taught the rapture of action. The ontology they founded recalled the story of Sisyphus: every time the stone rolls back down the hill. But is that any reason to abandon the stone at the foot of the mountain? Should we just sit back and watch the others as they go at it once more and laugh from the side of the road as once again they tackle the mountain? Should we just kick back on a pile of rubble? Why act rather than do nothing? The Claremont Road colony, the temporary residents of the TAZ, all of them were aware of the beautiful absurdity of the cause, however, unlike the dandies of the end times, they took up the fallen stone again and again, rolling it away from the foot of the mountain so that they would never again find themselves stuck there with the laughing ones at the side of the garbage heap.

Act II. I set out on my quest like a dowser—I
snatched up a hazel branch and I swept it to the right,
to the left, waved it in the direction of the poles,
towards Mecca . . . The branch had nothing good to tell
me. Were there still places left where the sealed world's
shrink-wrap was breached? Expecting nothing, I pointed my branch at the Americas, tracing a wide arc from
Tierra del Fuego to Alaska. To my great surprise, the
dowsing rod began to tremble . . . to the west . . . an
eruption! It had all the necessary characteristics: poetry,
the word, the sense of the fleeting, signs of magic. It did
not come from the power nexus. It had no link with any
major metropolis. Not San Francisco and its Haight-
Ashbury, nor Paris and its Latin Quarter, nor Rome, nor
Tokyo. The new insurrection was being born at the edge
of the world, in a distant jungle. In a forest that
recalled Rousseau's *Reveries*. A forest covered in the
same mists as Lamartine's *Lake*. A pagan forest, inhabited by spirits and strange creatures. A magical forest
next to a magic mountain where the primeval world
seemed to have found refuge. Chiapas. The same world
that Hoffmann described in *Little Zachary* "where the
most astonishing prodigies occur every day, and where
everyone, in this charming and delicious atmosphere of
enchantment, believed fully in the marvelous."[85] With
more than a century between them, it was the same land-
scape, the same lyricism directed at the same tragedy.
The enchanted forest was under attack, ravaged and dev-
astated. The word came to its aid by giving form to its
enchantments. "One fine day . . . Prince Paphnutius
decided that we would proclaim by decree the institution
of the Enlightenment: he commanded that the forests be

felled, the river dredged to make it navigable, that potatoes should be cultivated in the newly-cleared fields, and that everyone be vaccinated against smallpox."[86] Since the time of Hoffmann, we have had ample opportunities to witness such destruction. January 1, 1994. The Lacandone Forest. The Zapatista Indians, have you heard of them? No, not a thing. Give me a coffee, please. Is that another one of those guerilla groups from deepest darkest Latin America? Down there in Mexico, they're talking about this strange little rebellion. Are they armed? They claim that semantics is the best weapon of all. They've even been seen attacking a military encampment with paper airplanes. Are there a lot of them? There are a million Indians, but their ideas are drawing the attention of young people from all over the world. Do they have a leader? He asks to be called "Sub-Commander," out of irony. Apparently, he's very well-read and thinks *Don Quixote* is the greatest work of literature. Just what kind of man is this? They say he's ironic—irony and a sense of the tragic. This is what's in Act II: an insurgent Word surges forth from a faraway jungle to put the last men to shame and awaken our visionary souls.

> In sum, we are an army of dreamers, and therefore invincible. How can we fail to win, with this imagination overturning everything. Or rather, we do not deserve to lose.[87]

The Zapatista movement is an example of lucid romanticism: It talks magic, but it knows what's real and what isn't. It responds to the law of scarcity by mourning abundance. It defends lyricism against the cold logics of capital. It rejects the atrophied existence of the citizens of rationality, consumers, and calculators. Like all of the romantics of the 19th century, Marcos tore himself away from despair. His writings alternate constantly between doubt and fervor. They do not call for literature to line up behind a political program. On the contrary, they seek to restore poetry to politics. Language comes alive in them, flows, bleeds, even blows its nose between parentheses. The style of their communiques, their laws, the decrees of the Ejercito Zapatista de Liberacion National express a feeling that is light-years away from the dried-up statistics of our Universal Political Economy and its glacial regulations, its ratios and curves and averages that end up reducing us to mere agents of production and consumption. The Zapatistas spoke out in the name of five hundred disastrous years of history, the years since the discovery of America. We however, heard a new sound, something fresh, something just taken out of a precious sleeve. We had never heard anything like it, it was beautiful, surprising, unimaginable. That such a voice could appear from out of the jungle, in the midst of laughter. Marcos cited *Don Quixote*, and we understood. In the closed world of capitalism after the Berlin Wall, Sancho Panza and the Knight of the Sad Face merged into one figure, and it resembled us. Time and time again, with our eyes wide open, without illusions, knowing that the cause was in vain, and that the struggle was a thing of the past, we would awake to find ourselves dreamers once again, devoted to an ideal the entire world had given up for dead and buried. The age of chivalry and the middle ages were the first historical period that the German romantics of the end of the 18th century identified with. Friedrich Schlegel taught us that it was the wellspring of romanticism, that it was from this "time of knights, of courtly love, of the story that the phenomenon and the word itself was derived."[88] After two centuries of horror, twenty years of co-optation, of about-faces, of abdication, we can no longer take the code of chivalry seriously. We are condemned to the intermittence of the ideal. Our wills must learn to be happy with little victories. Like Don Quixote, we were not of our own times, and in this time warp, the flows of capital seemed to us giants even more invincible than windmills. "Absurdities of the sea, some will say. It is of no importance, we keep sailing all the same."[89]

I was not surprised to learn that *Don Quixote* had a place on Marcos's nightstand. Quixote embodied the great figure of rebellion after the Great Confinement in the 17th century. The naiveté of the character combined with the lucidity of the narrator. It was given to us to be both simultaneously. And from this marriage was born a superior form of ridicule. Let the cynics laugh and fade away laughing. Let the snide turn up their noses at us. Let the dandies humiliate us. Each time we emerged stronger and even more resolute. Maybe we were anachronisms, but we were sublime. We wrote the book and then jumped out of the book, talking to you. We were the stage directors of our own lost causes. The mockers and the hecklers were simply spectators. Spectators! Get this right—spectators means critics and deconstructors, that is to say, impotent voyeurs. That's the corner that cynical rationality backed itself into, imagining that criticism was superior to action. It decided that laughter was superior to tears, decided it could prevail against feeling by rendering itself insensible. Marcos's passion for *Don Quixote* interrupted this pose, and I believe that it is in this sense and in this sense only, that his insurrection was a revolution. An act of self-overcoming. Because it dared to dramatize rather than simply announce the aspirations of the Zapatistas, and so the spectator was put in his place. The Zapatista reality went so far outside of the conventional frame of reference that the critics of the frame were thrown into disarray. Beyond the simulacrum, beyond fiction, beyond the image—the innocent lucidity of the Zapatista poem demonstrated that now it was possible to mock the mockers, to laugh at laughter, and through this irony, to take action in the name of a stirring ideal.

As early as a week after the insurrection, sympathizers gathered in the most famous squat of the New York underground: ABC NO RIO.[90] One of their number, Ricardo Dominguez, a self-professed "theater person who hated theater," was part of an artists' collective with its roots in Tallahassee, Florida: The Critical Art Ensemble. In the 80s, CAE members fought together with Act-Up Miami against the indifference of the "Therapeudic State" and the maneuvering of the big pharmaceutical laboratories. Like it always happens, at the end of the road, they came face to face with THE GREATEST PROBLEM OF THE AGE—the same problem that I see as one of the five pillars of our new confinement: how do you confront a power that is no longer of this world? Their essay, *Electronic Disturbance* (1990) attempted to formulate an answer. It was published by Autonomedia, Hakim Bey's publisher. After the opening made by the TAZ, the tactic presented by the CAE cut another swath in the walls of our resignation: since power had evaporated, we too should begin boiling. Not to reach the fluidity of the *skeeze*, but to transform ourselves into fine particles of water vapor, and thus infiltrate the gears of power, leaving behind our rust. A sentient rust! A rust to make the clever machinery of dematerialized capital seize up. A virtual rust to call back to mind the other rust, that melancholy rust of obsolete machine tools and old factory hands. At that time, the tools of the electronic struggle were still fairly crude, but its language was already fully formed:

> Elite power, having rid itself of its national and urban bases to wander in absence on the electronic pathways, can no longer be disrupted by strategies predicated upon the contestation of sedentary forces. The architectural monuments of power are hollow and empty, and function now only as bunkers for the complicit and those who acquiesce. They are secure places revealing mere traces of power . . . These places can be occupied, but to do so will not disrupt the nomadic flow . . . The avant-garde never gives up, and yet the limitations of antiquated models and the sites of resistance tend to push resistance into the void of disillusionment.[91]

The unions watched helplessly as plant closure followed plant closure. The European socialist parties clamored to show that they too understood the laws of the market. In the cities, most people let themselves go, feeding the ranks of *mass dandyism*. The CAE, however were enlisting digital pirates to bring the ethereal flux back down to earth. With the exception of certain Sci-Fi authors, they were the first theorists of electronic civil disobedience. "Just as authority located in the street was once met by demonstrations and barricades, the authority that locates itself in the electronic field must be met with electronic resistance . . . Nomadic power must be resisted in cyberspace rather than in physical space."

The writings of the CAE marked a consciousness in transition—they represent the moment when the hackers were called on to join the resistance. The Finnish philosopher Pikka Himanen, a researcher at UC Berkeley, showed that from its earliest days in the 70s, there was already a conflict between capitalist and hacker ethics at the heart of the electronic revolution. While the former thought of work as a duty, profit as a distinction, acquiring and amassing wealth as hallmarks of personal worth, the latter ethic is based on play, pleasure, and sharing.[92] For a long time this opposition remained silent. Its demonstrations came only late. Up until the middle of the 90s, the hacker community kept out of politics. Ricardo called that tendency *digitally correct hacking*—hackers who mainly cared about free access to code—and contrasted them to *digitally incorrect hackers* who were concerned with putting the means offered by the digital revolution at the service of a concrete political cause. During the entire 80s, the hackers defended the 0 and the 1 as the universal language, a kind of biblical return to an era before Babel where the most remote populations were able to exchange knowledge. They formed a community without borders, the first diaspora founded neither on history, nor on blood. The only bond they shared was technology and the information they passed on to each other through snail mail to improve their machine. It was this lack of commitment that the CAE criticized.

Ricardo Dominguez's encounter with the Zapatista movement in New York at the beginning of 1994 was typical of the emergence of the new dissident consciousness: dispersed local activist groups began to *resonate* with one another remotely, through elective affinities or empathy. Gradually, with the aid of technology, they pulled themselves out of their corners and shuffled off their anonymity to reach an autonomous stage of organization. The I produced a WE. On January 1, 1994, the day of the uprising, the Zapatistas penetrated the digital commons by sending out by email the first declaration of the Lacandone Jungle. Within five days, thousands of digital Zapatistas appeared on the Net. The group Ya Basta! was created in Italy, while in Mexico, Ricardo launched the New York Community for Democracy. I have often read that the Seattle meeting in November 1999 was the crucible of a new dissident movement, and I guess that's what the history books will say. Nevertheless, the emergence of the *hyperconsciousness* that made it possible had already occurred—it was already gestating at Claremont Road, in the jungle at Lacandone, in New York at ABC NO RIO and among the members of Ya Basta! in Italy. At each stage, a thought, a technological platform, and the quiverings of a network of inspiration. It was not a scheduled coming-together, but a somewhat provisory assemblage of exchanges all of them searching for tactics that could tear us from our confinement and despair.

In the dispatches of the CAE, just like in those sent from the jungle of Lacandone, you saw over and over again the same intuitions: henceforth, the Word would be mightier than weapons. The struggle was shifting from three-dimensional space to semantic space.[93] "That's how the Zapatistas became the main infowar community online," Ricardo told me. "Because they grasped that the dialectic of the 21st century was no longer based on materialism but on semantics. Semantics is the main aspect of the information war. That is to say, not words for war, but words as war." The infowar was nothing more than a reformulation of the conflict between our poetic essence and the commercial being. Electronic realities were the continuation of shamanic realities. Both authorized the grafting of dreams to reality. This multitude of strata, this thousand-layer pancake of visions. The truth is, the *new incarnation* sought by *lucid romanticism* was nothing more than a renaissance—our magical depths took over the networks. That was our key to understanding why the slogan "We are all Zapatista Indians" was so successful. It was more than just an expression of sympathy: We are . . . I am . . . Identity . . . Identification . . . We are magical because we are electronic. Cyberspace could serve as a pasture for our memories much better than it could be the playground of the *skeeze*. It authorized us to be a thousand different characters, have a thousand different avatars. Through it, we could be the Word incarnate of the body's here and the virtual Word of the beyond.

"The inhabited area of the forest was the place of the dead, of ghosts, of all the stories that still dwell in the night of the forest of Lacandone."[94]

Behind the Great Green Gate . . .

Act III. Towards the middle of the 90s, bodies began to reappear, and with them, the idea of space, of matter, and all the dimensions of humanity. Argentine *piqueteros*, Brazilian homeless, urban resistance fighters from New York, travelers, ravers and modern English nomads, *sans-droits* in France, and then the Italian *Tute Bianchi*. Not all of these movements responded to the same crises. Still, the bodies they mobilized all sought to take back space and make their presence felt against the *invisibility* and *fluidity* to which the market wanted to consign them. To do this, they came up with a sleight of hand thing, an abstraction even more abstract than capital itself. An abstraction of an abstraction. An aesthetic that would make Malevitch blush. The white square on a white background of dissidence. A project that had begun at Chiapas, developed in France with the jobless movement, and which then reached Italy: make the invisible visible. This was what the third act of the new incarnation was all about. After the deconstruction of despair and the semantic renaissance, the dance of the *Invisibles* against the empire of flows.[95]

I discovered the condition of the invisible at a very tender age. In Calcutta . . . Bengal, India. I have family there. My great-aunt, whose name is Krishna, was born there. She's an aristocrat, a descendant of the honorable Rabindranath Tagore, the Nobel laureate for literature. Très Chic. My great-aunt is dead, but the family has kept her mother's house. Inside, there is an immense bed, a moustiquaire, two faded photos by Henri Cartier-Bresson that date from the time he stayed here, two French doors through which the murmur of the city secretly filters, a low table, a commode. Everything sits on a cement floor painted a red-ochre. The living room has an odor of dust: portraits of ancestors, another low table, and a silence accented by the blades of an old fan that only stirs up memories. The kitchen is empty, the emptiness of premodern times. Around my great-aunt's house in Calcutta, there is also a garden, and to guard the garden, a great green gate. Behind the great green gate, the mass of *Invisibles*. We know the tune, *the poor of Calcutta*. So intensely has the gaze of the West eroticized their sunken cheeks and bellies, so completely has Mother Theresa sanctified their dispossession, then in the end we envy them. The *poor of Calcutta* . . . clichés. Images without value, vehicles for ostentatious compassion. At first, it looks pretty, then one loses the desire to see, then finally, the power to see. Take it from me, I felt it like a spike in the eye. In Calcutta, in front of the house of my great-aunt, beyond the immense bed, the mousquitaire, the old fan, the two low tables, the red-ochre cement, and the French doors, beyond the great green gate, the *Invisible One* is visible. He is visible because he stinks. He lives because he stinks. And this stink pierces your eyes and knocks it into your skull that that bodies cannot be reduced to flows. It was to remind the *skeezes* of that stench that in the 90s the diaspora of resistance forged the aesthetic of the *Invisibles*.

The first emblem of this aesthetic was the mask. Not the kind of mask you wear in Venice on carnival nights. The illegal mask. A ski mask. A swatch of fabric. Scratchy wool, runny eyes and nose. Breath that heats up the cheeks. Irritated cheeks. From one side of the Atlantic to the other, from the political world to the world of music, from insurrection to rave, the Invisible wore a mask to make its presence felt. The Zapatistas were masked. The musicians of Underground Resistance also. The first rose up the day that NAFTA came into force. Others sought to escape the control of record labels. In each case, though, the mask was the invisible bodies' answer to the abstractions of the flows. In Chiapas and Detroit, the dissident consciousness was already learning about the game of appearances: there is no control without identity, and no identity without a face. When you hide the face, you dissolve identity and elude the procedures of control. The mask was that eraser. A form of protection. A way of responding to the image, not by criticism or dry manipulations, but by dissimulating and the preservation of innocence. Here, I would have liked to toss in some glib quotations from my courses on *The Birth of Tragedy* and tell how dissimulating always breeds excesses and strength, and also how the masks of the insurgents and the underground parties were a thumb in the eye of the simple system of signification of market exchange. Tell how, finally, from the forests of England to the Lacandone jungle, the mask heralded the return of Dionysus to the arena of Apollo. Alas, I burned all my notes the day after I finished my final high school exams. Bye Antigone. Bye Sophocles. Bye Nietzsche . . . I gave a name to this little ceremony: *the kindling of the idols*. These weren't flames of disgust, but rather flames of joy. I figured that now that I was done with school, the world would leave me alone. I regretted it later—why go and burn up your archives? I might have plunged back into them and distilled a theory from them: a comparative study of the mask in Greek drama and the ski-mask of the Chiapas indians. Pretty lame. What did you learn during all these years? What ever became of all your ponderings? The mask, for God's sake! Why did it pop up outside of these old theaters? I thought its fate was sealed. Simulacra of partying—the Gay Pride Parade— had emptied it of its Dionysian charge. Its multiple meanings had been smuggled out of Africa and sold to the highest bidder. In fact, not at all! The mask was not dead. On the contrary, it was alive with the full robust life of the dead.

The mask was reborn to escape the confinement of the image. The mask was reborn to escape the confinement of identity. The mask was reborn to escape the cheapening of meaning. The mask was reborn to save the ones excluded from the empire of flows. The mask was reborn because politics had become a charade in which we no longer cared to participate unmasked. Once it had served to give the supernatural flesh. Now it gave a face to the world's faceless, to those who refused to play along, to the dropouts, to the wretched, capitalism's dejected and rejected. Like the pseudonym, the mask was the only worthwhile strategy of resistance versus the transformation of the poets among us into admen. The age of dissimulation versus the age of promotion.

The body that was reborn with the mask had learned something from the raves of the 90s. It was neither blasé, nor bored, nor committed. It was a secret body, hidden, camouflaged, provisionally out of this world rather than melancholically against the world. In his book *Senseless Acts of Beauty*,[96] George McKay took care to point out that in the beginning, raves were not directly political. On the contrary, they were the result of an encounter between Thatcherian individualism, the hedonism of Club Med, the resurgence, without the revolutionary aura, of psychedelic drug use (e.g. esctasy instead of acid), and a technological cyber-optimism. That said, the docile body of the raver was laid hold of in the midst of its escapist capers—the state refused to countenance even this behavior. It moved to stop them. It denied them access to space. In 1994, the British Parliament passed a law that swiftly repoliticized this group: the Criminal and Justice Act, typical of similarly named laws. It had every insoluble nomad, every raver and traveler, explicitly in its sights. On the basis of articles 63, 64, and 65, underground parties were outlawed: "A 'rave' is defined as a gathering of 100 plus people, at which amplified music is played which is likely to cause serious distress to the local community, in the open air and at night. These sections give the police the power to order people to leave the land if they're believed to be: Preparing to hold a rave (two or more people); Waiting for a rave to start (10 or more); Actually attending a rave (10 or more)." Apollo gained some ground. The occupation of land—even if it was common property—was criminalized, and so explicitly that the ravers were lifted out of their apathy. And the same thing could be seen taking place all over. The capital flows were seeking to irradiate every bit of space-time, and bodies everywhere abruptly stood up as straight as the cock on a hanged man. You know how when the trapdoor of the gallows drops down and the rope brutally squeezes the neck of the condemned, his blood rushes to his head and his dick suddenly gets hard. Mechanically. By colonizing new spaces, capital extended the battlefield and transformed what until then had just been a desire to exist into a necessity to resist. Like a militant in the cold pale dawn, it tore us away from our dreams. By piercing flesh and irradiating space, it tried to force matter and spirit to fold themselves up and then dissolve . . . And it is against this same dissolution-vanishing that the Indians of Chiapas had begun their own resistance, against the same disincarnation that the English activists of Reclaim the Streets continued the struggle begun at Claremont Road, against this lack of anywhere to run that the ravers awoke from their trances.

I had just finished my studies for good. Two of the best schools. I figured that I left school behind without major damage, with a clear conscience. Today I recognize I was wrong. What in France we call the *Grandes Écoles* mark you even more distinctly than bad perfume. It takes years to wash that off you. The learning, the old-boy networks, the complacency, comes together around you like a net in spite of yourself to catch you one day or another at the fork in some road. The best schools leave you beaten, dazed, the mind soft as mud. *Culture générale*, general culture, is their awful name for lobotomy. It takes a lot of strength to wrench yourself from the destiny that they have planned for you. A lot of courage to keep from giving up and retain a sense of wonder. One might think that it's nothing compared to the fate of the crowd, but the fate of the crowd, precisely depends on these schools, these idea-factories and the representations they pass on, the concepts they want to engrain in your mind. The only pride that I retain from this experience is that when I was there, I had two thousand chances to become an idiot, and yet I did not. In the libraries of the best schools, nothing is off limits, there arc no special access collections. They have but one objective and one function: save the Institution. "What is a citizen?" "French monetary policy in doubt?" "Whither, Europe?" "American foreign policy, 1945–1989," "Developing Countries," etc. The *Grandes Écoles* make the consensus. They erect a holy image of a representative, centrist democracy, blind to the huge heap of abstentions that invalidates it. Thesis, antithesis, prosthesis . . . You sit for long hours in a lecture hall. You dream of a university where one learns to think the way one carves wood. But no! The wood is the wood of a stable where one force-feeds pigs. Around you, students flatter themselves that they have adult views. Little moldable miniatures so glad to be molded by the guardians of bitterness. After you've been through all that, it's easier to understand why from England to Tierra del Fuego governments sell and auction off their people . . . citizen-consumers . . . mud-wallowers speaking to mud-wallowers . . .

I left the London School of Economics for New York. I stayed there for a few months. This is the way we build our stores, build our stores, build our stores . . . the East more and more resembled the West. Investment was overtaking the real. In the trilogy of TAZ, anti-TAZ, and synTAZ, we were closest to an anti-TAZ period. The state and the multinationals continued their great spring cleaning. Decidedly, the operation to stigmatize the invisible bodies was not going to be accomplished with a magic wand, like making a rabbit in a hat vanish, but rather with a club. Everywhere, the magic trick followed the same well-defined logic: marginal populations were criminalized. Their wanderings were forbidden. Trucks were sent out to pick up what John Major referred to as municipal waste. City authorities favored commerce and servicing the tourist, while driving away insolvent nomads.

Was it an irony of history or simple coincidence that on January 1, 1994, the date of the Zapatista insurrection, Rudolph Giuliani, who would quickly acquire the nickname "Adolph," started his first term as New York's mayor? I know that it's hard to go back and imagine the feelings he inspired at that time. In the heat of the crisis that hit America on 9/11, the U.S. recognized him as one of their heroes. *Time* declared him Man of the Year. Strange amnesia! For me, for us, the children of the double collapse, Rudy was first and foremost the great demographic cleanser, the inventor of zero tolerance, of a security- and hygiene-oriented urban policy that if it failed to change the world, at least severely disfigured Manhattan. He called it the economic reconquest of the old city centers. Before our very eyes, New York was transformed into a giant Disneyland. The Times Square beloved of Henry Miller vanished. Police brutality was accepted as the inevitable price of crime fighting. Whether you call him Rudy, Giuliani, or Adolph, my hope is to one day see him taken down from his pedestal to receive the epitaph he deserves: 1994–2001, Mayor of Gotham, Epic Cleanser. His "broken windows" theory that won the support of police worldwide held that the most innocuous graffitti tag should be treated as the first danger sign of pervasive decadence. If you want to eliminate crime, then you must eliminate poetry. Fucking Giuliani. And they revere you! Explain it to the whores, to the billy-clubbed winos, to the invisibles and their stench of pussy and alcohol. The bleach of commercial hygiene versus the bleach-like odor of sperm. Thanks to it, the theater of our wanderings has been remade as a shopping mall. The city has been sold. Sold, the scarred facades. Sold, our nostalgia. One prostitution drives out the other. The police protected private interests while the private interests remolded the heart of the city into something new. Mickey Mouse, a Big Mac, a cookie at Starbucks, and the check please. Capital was victorious over the biggest TAZ in the world—Manhattan. Rudy as the antithesis of the TAZ, our anti-TAZ, holding off the syn-TAZ, the Saint TAZ. Dionysus crucified.

The aesthetic of the *Invisibles*, based on the dissimulation of identity and the reincarnation of bodies, developed in response to this program. It represented the rejection of absorption and the reincarnation of bodies. The broken mirror of faces and the stench of the flesh. It taught rootedness, attachment to place, the defense of space. It called for the establishment of a city of drifters. The city I loved, after all. With gaps, enclaves in transition. The city as jungle, as a chaotic ecosystem—neighborhood movie theaters, Fellinian cities versus Wal-Mart-led developments. Cities of Mystery à la Nerval and floating cities à la Rimbaud. Should we have been ashamed of this nostalgia? A nostalgia that would once again dare to shout: "Long live crime! Long live crime! Long live crime!" Nostalgia for *that*? Rudy was our Napoleon, the rule-maker, the conqueror, the guy who took his mission of law and order everywhere, and like Pontalis's French Civil Code, transformed vagabonds into mental patients, filled the night with checkpoints, cleaned up the streets, shut down the haunts of pleasure-seekers. The middle class citizen in whose name he legislated did not wear a top hat and a pocket watch. He sported a walkman, trainers, and a blazer on Fridays, and smelled of mentholated after-shave. Brett Easton Ellis's *American Psycho* had replaced the banker Lafitte. Consumer hygiene had replaced the ethics of thrift. Nevertheless, the bourgeois plucked out winos' eyeballs and murdered hookers to assuage his hatred of his body.

Like the post-romantics Stendhal, Flaubert, and Balzac, we studied at the school of disenchantment. The rules of capitalism, books on microeconomics, restructuring plans, the annual reports of multinational corporations, the laws of supply and demand . . . this was our Encyclopedia Britannica, our National Geographic, our book of whys and wherefores. Like the post-romantics, there was not enough space in the reality we inherited to hold our dreams. In France, they lived through the Empire, then the Restoration—first Napoleon, then Charles X. From the front row, they watched pushy newcomers change regimes like shirts. Whether the shirts had lace collars or not made little difference. Since then, we have gone from the cynical social climbing of Balzac's Rastignac to *mass dandyism*, but the resignation has remained identical from Talleyrand to Mitterand, trait for trait . . . you have to think that even with a century between them, kids who grow up listening to the same tale react to it with the same passions. He wants to flee this world of petty opportunists. He believes first of all in a mist-shrouded forest, but soon the mists will not be enough. So he puts down his Lamartine, his Musset and his Hugo, finding them too maudlin, too desperate, too patriotic. He sinks his teeth savagely into the real, to describe with greatness the world of pettynesses. Hello, Balzac, hey there, Flaubert, *come stai*, Stendahl? Romanticism + realism, hope + despair, the outside + the temporary. Just as the rationality of the Enlightenment thinkers and the intrigues of the European cities provoked a romantic response in the 18th and then in the 19th centuries, the rationality of capital and the vanity of the *skeezes* at the end of the 20th and beginning of the 21st century have awoken THE GREAT "I" OF POETIC CRITICISM. "I" IS "WE" IN WORLD INCARNATE WHERE DIMENSION REPLACES THE FLUID AS THE NEW MODERNITY. "I" IS PERIPHERAL, DROPS OUT TO PROTECT ITS INNOCENCE, BUT "I" KNOWS EVERYTHING ABOUT THE RESIGNA-TION AND CYNICISM THAT LURKS EVERY-WHERE, AND SO "I" IS THE ARCH-MOCKER AT THE HEART OF THE WORLD . . . BUT FROM ONE ENCLAVE TO ANOTHER, "I" BUMPS INTO THOU-SANDS OF OTHERS AND THEIR PERCUSSIONS FORM THE GREAT PAGAN "WE" OF THE NEW INCARNATION.

Party at Ikea Tonight!

Act IV. I entered the real world, as one says. School was over, no more teachers, no more exams. So long, hormones! Soon, I could get myself a bed. Soon, I'd stagger home from work each night exhausted. I would turn on the TV. I would watch the helpless submarine *Kursk* sink to the sea floor, like the little girl in the mud, from when I was five years old. I'd snack on peanuts and make cocktails. A dried-up raisin for my dried-up reason. Soon, I'd be enjoying the spectacle of the mud-wallowers' ball. Soon, I'd be just like all the elite, mesmerized by court dramas at the tiny center of the world. I'd watch insignificant intrigues unfold, keep tabs on who was in favor and who was out. Will we still be in the lineup next season? Human resource departments, career guidance counselors. Are you a people person? What about PR? Soon, I'd send a resume and a cover letter in a bid to replace one of the victims of the World Trade Center. I didn't fit the description of the ideal candidate. Soon, I'd call up my old friends in PR. I'd apologize for having treated them with such contempt. After all, they had a family, a respectable job, a sensible pension fund. They tell me yes!—they'd call if something come up. Then they'd tell me to just wait a bit—wait until the economy picks up a bit, wait until the outlook improves. I'd hang up, shaken by the movers and shakers. Just a few more days and it'd be an extreme makeover. Profoundly moved, I'd soberly consider the follies of my youth. I'd take steps to live down this reputation as a politically-engaged young man. Yeah, right. What are you talking about? C'mon. I don't believe in a-ny-thing. How could I? I'd renounce the age of acne. I'd mellow with age. I'd become a writer, an artist, a creator of something—in any event, something impressive, something that impresses you, something you read about in the press. I'd use my status to enflame the hearts of those younger than me. Sometimes so young that it'd be a scandal. I'd defend this elevated lust in order to freshen up the slightly *demodé* subversiveness of my image. I wouldn't be bitter. For I'd realize, after all, that rebellion and revolt are never anything more than pretexts; excuses to sweep away the remnants of a worn-out world and let in some sun. I wouldn't convince anyone . . . but I had tried to tell it how it is.

I was still young. I wasn't even twenty-three years old. I'd built some solid networks. Dissidence was an excellent racket. Without really meaning to, I became a sort of pizza delivery man of subversive thought, a FreshDirect of the counterculture, the Meals On Wheels of the offbeat, the Cheesy Crust of revolt. The deeper I touched rebel souls, the wider the grin on my banker's face. So how is our anger doing today, sir? And my bank account, how is *it* doing? Very well, sir. Better and better. Wonderfully. Would you like some funds? Well, why not? After all. It's very nice indeed to reconstruct one's long-lost uterus in a larger version, with a few club chairs scattered about. Ikea's open late every Thursday night. They have a little party. Oh, too bad, I'm hosting a show on melancholy and the future. I won't be able to make it. Another time, maybe. Yes! Another time . . . the world all but set a course for me. If I read something, it had to be something USEFUL. If I took a piss, it had to be a USEFUL piss. If I went out, it was work. USEFUL. If I danced, it had to be a USEFUL dance. If I smiled, it had to be a USEFUL smile. And all the while, my head was literally pounding with these words: when will I ever be able to read USELESSLY, piss USELESSLY, dance USELESSLY, and smile USELESSLY? To protect the innocents, I never went anywhere without a pseudonym. One name one place, another name somewhere else. An exploded identity, an identity in pieces, so as not to be the ONE that knows how and the one that tells how at the same time. In the end, I dreamt of abstinence, of holing up somewhere by myself. But then there is always the telephone. Its always ringing. It's there. It follows me. In the Tangier medina. That mosquito sound in the middle of nowhere. In that restaurant in La Bocca in Buenos Aires . . . on vibrate so as not to disturb El Chino, the owner, who sings tangos sad enough to tear you in two. The waves rippling in your pocket, against your thigh, bring you back down to earth again, back into the active world, back to work, back into the flux. And there you are again, inside. Completely inside. I watch these *new wave* dissidents find their place in the world. Rebellion finally becomes a job like any other, it just boils down to who is going to sit on the left of the host and who is going to sit on the right. OK, you with the beard, girly-man, liberal, scream! Scream louder! C'mon, go for it! The bigger the fight, the better the ratings . . . and as for you, you realists who say you have practical solutions, reforms to suggest . . . go on, go ahead. Relax. One day it will all be included in the GREAT REFORM. Inside. On the interior. We watched the generation of the 60s become captains of industry. We watched the punks become consultants. And we'll end up just like them. Unless . . .

> We have to come up with a new concept, critical unrealism, to denote the opposition of an imaginary ideal, utopian and marvelous universe to the grey, prosaic and inhuman reality of the modern world . . . It's by their critically unreal character that not only writers and poets like Novalis and Hoffmann, but also utopian thinkers and revolutionaries like Charles Fourier, Moss Hess and William Morris brought an essential dimension to romanticism, one as worthy of attention as the uncompromisingly realist lucidity of a Balzac or a Dickens . . . At each turn of events, romanticism split into progressive and reactionary currents.[97]

This is were we stood. The old has not yet sloughed off from the new. The reactionary was still inseparable from the modern. Just like at the turn of the 19th century. Madame de Staël—in *Of Germany*, the book that's always cited as marking the emergence of French Romanticism—was not yet completely free from the influence of the Enlightenment. In his *The Genius of Christianity*, Chateaubriand spoke in the name of the exiles from the monarchy's golden age. Both of them hesitated. More modern than the ancients, more nostalgic than the moderns. The awakening of sentiment called for the body and its dimensions to be brought back from oblivion, yet it was still flirting with the world of the past. All of romanticism's ambiguity is right there. It's up to its contemporaries to toss it in the basement with the rest of the old things or raise it high in the skies among utopian dreams. We were at a similar historical point at the turn of this century. The hesitation stage. A passing phase. On the side of the old, the Cassandras of the National Idea. On the new, us! Unreasonable wanderers in an antibody era, antiearth, antiflesh, hiding ourselves out of timidity, joyous because we were desperate, at home with our bodies, but without borders, ironic because unsure, nostalgic not of the past that is no more, but for a future that *could* be. All this agitation, could it have led us anywhere else other than where it did?

Lucid romanticism staggered. Determined to rediscover the body and the blood and the earth, sometimes it found itself on the side of reactionaries and sometimes it ended up with the paranoids. It had not yet touched the heart of the times and altered the point of view of its contemporaries. It said pretty things, but its voice did not persuade. What happened was that at the heart of the world, *mass dandyism* and the *skeezes* heard nothing. Art. Yes! Only art and literature could save the dimension of being and spirituality, only they could rise above historical passion, attain the real, slice it up and conquer other minds until the confinement was shattered by death or by liberty, and the body reappeared, battered and bloodied by the flux, but victorious.

At the beginning of 1998, I got mail. It was from the Electronic Disturbance Theater, a group of NYC activists and Zapatista sympathizers founded by Ricardo Dominguez. They were organizing a virtual demonstration against the Mexican government. Two members of EDT, Carmin Karasic and Brett Stalbaum, had borrowed one of the first pieces of virtual demonstration software from Italian hackers: Netstrike, the program already used against the resumption of French nuclear testing. It had since been renamed Floodnet. Links between indian peasants in a hidden corner of Mexico, hip hacktivists on the American east coast, Italian social housing centers, and TAZs the world over were now possible. The new incarnation became part of the network age. The EDT's action was followed by the Acteal massacre of Chiapas, in which forty-five Indians were killed. In just a few months, solidarity emails and websites turned the traditional means of struggle on its head. A whole constellation of pockets of resistance were henceforth resonating with one another. They supported each other, kept eachother informed, helped eachother. To me they resembled the pirate archipelagos that plagued the great shipping routes in the 15th and 16th centuries. There was the island of underground partiers, who had survived the neoliberal assault of Margaret Thatcher, the Italian squatters of the social housing movement, where the radical left had holed up, the Situationist pie-throwers hibernating in Belgium, the first digital activists, save few recalcitrant artists who refused to admire themselves in the mirror of merchandise. There were also the gay and lesbian movements, the minority groups in the U.S., the eco-warriors, and finally, enlightened members of the managerial class fighting for their ideals from within NGOs. All of these archipelagos comprised a dissident *hyperconsciousness* and this hyperconsciousness now began to stir:

> The sea-rovers and corsairs of the 18th century created an "information network" that spanned the globe: primitive and devoted primarily to grim business, the net nevertheless functioned admirably. Scattered throughout the net were islands, remote hideouts where ships could be watered and provisioned, booty traded for luxuries and necessities. Some of these islands supported "intentional communities," whole mini-societies living consciously outside the law and determined to keep it up, even if only for a short but merry life.[98]

In contrast to the earlier romanticism, the one now being born liked to point to piracy more often than to the middle ages. Operating outside the law was in the parlance of the times called civil disobedience, but there was a form of activity that remained intact. Contempt for borders, dissidence vis-à-vis the state, competition with the legitimate authorities. The myth of chivalry and the image of Don Quixote were left behind in favor of the great buccaneers of the Renaissance: Jean Ango, Jean Fleury, Jacques de Sores, and François Clerc, a.k.a. Pegleg. After having deterritorialized itself in order to persuade the pirates of digital space, the resistance came back to earth . . . or rather back to sea. Because the representatives of power concealed themselves on ships and sailed from port to port—or rather from airport to airport—but so did the pirates' privateers chasing them to their next temporary residence. Seattle, Davos, Prague, Nice, Québec, Gotheburg, Genoa . . . this is how the nomad processions came together, this *trans-resistance*. The era of Russian dolls, of cascading hourglasses, of deferred accountability was attacked head-on. The *trans-resistance* followed a double movement. It became fluid in order to confront fluid power. It coalesced and became momentarily incarnate to grapple with the incarnation of power. It had created mobile temples for its members and was completely unconstrained by the framework of nation-states. So long, parliamentary democracy. The sentient beings were elsewhere, in the streets of other cities, in the countryside of other lands. They had grasped that true sovereignty was to be found in this wandering, borderless organization, that it was the carrier of poetic legitimacy. This was the form of theater that could return power to the human will *as a part* of History. And it is the edification of these temporary temples that makes the historical expression of *lucid romanticism* and its pirate dialectic possible.

This is how I understood the slogan *Another world is possible*. At first, it made me smile. Always this smirk crawling over my lips. I said to myself, "Another world? okay, but what world?" The slogan had the air of all those quaint phrases from the arsenal of utopianism. Nevertheless, I forced myself to listen to it without laughing, so that it rang out not *piano* but *forte*. You have to take hope seriously. Of course, the managers of dissidence do have some concrete proposals as well: the Tobin Tax, debt forgiveness, the privileging of the "good" principles of international law over commerce. All of the various bold plans dreamed up by the partisans of antiglobalization and altermondialism. Secretely, however, I know that these ideas all have another objective beyond themselves. Their economic realism is secondary to their real inspiration. The pirate dialectic is of another order. It opposes what the writer Robert Musil magnificently described as the *sense* of the real and the *sense* of the possible. Like Ulrich, Musil's protagonist in *The Man Without Qualities*, the *lucid romantics* are partisans of the possible. That's what makes them different from the romantics of the past. They doubt more than they believe. They prefer to explore rather than to draw conclusions. They open more than they close. They embrace more than they exclude. It is the indefiniteness of the other world that we are trying to reach, and the affirmation of this right to search for it that is the linchpin of the *trans-resistance*. The dialectic that it is creating is indeterminate. It seeks to provoke the real rather than to replace it. Musil writes:

> So the sense of possibility could be defined outright as the ability to conceive of everything there might be just as well, and to attach no more importance to what is than to what is not. The consequences of so creative a disposition can be remarkable, and may, regrettably, often make what people admire seem wrong, and what is taboo permissible, or, also, make both a matter of indifference . . . Such possibilists are said to inhabit a more delicate medium, a hazy medium of mist, fantasy, daydreams, and the subjunctive mood. Children who show this tendency are dealt with firmly and warned that such persons are cranks, dreamers, weaklings, know-it-alls, or troublemakers . . . [99]

We the children of the double collapse, all of us *were that child*, the one that was "dealt with firmly" in an effort to get rid of its sense of the possible. We learned to just laugh at it all. The *spirit of endings* very nearly convinced us that abdication was the only way to go. We used the critique of the Spectacle to launch critical spectacles. We were competent, versed in the thousand little tricks that make one a good columnist, an excellent writer-editor, subtly urbane, and fiercely hip, happy *skeezes*, in short. We were that child for we were on the verge of taking up the pose of resignation. Today we have the choice between two ways of existing. The first "wants the forest, as it were, and the other the trees," wrote Musil. While cynicism is the dominant trait of the partisans of the real, the "possibilists" have resolved to dig themselves out of resignation. I want to underline that this is only a general tendency, because in the marches in Seattle, Prague, and Genoa, I saw that there was an infinite variety of ways that the *spirit of endings* came very close to convincing us to abandon hope. There were the Black Blocs, the groups closest to despair. Then the rosy disobedience of the Pinks, the closest to laughter. The white of the *Tute Bianchi*, halfway between irony and despair. *Lucid romanticism* covered the entire spectrum of feelings. Its rebellion still bore the scars of past defeats within it, but a common faith united it and lifted it out of resignation: the faith in elegance.

As I finish this book, I am twenty-four years old. Carlo Giuliani was twenty-one when he died at Genoa on July 20, 2001. The rear window of the jeep was broken, and from that window the *carabiniere* opened fire. Carlo Giuliani approached the jeep. He had a ski-mask on and brandished a fire extinguisher. "I heard bang! bang! And the young man fell to the ground. A geyser of blood spouted from his eye. I knew he was dead right away." It was a tragic error, they said. The *carabinere* got scared. He was young. Carlo Giuliani was young too. I do not think that he planned on dying for the G8, but I'll bet that he had thought about dying for all the rest—to exit this world of impossibility, to be no longer doomed to resignation, to not have to adopt the cynical laugh of the spectacle, finally, to not be like the rest of us, beings suffocating on the inside of a huge glass cage. He broke a window before dying. The window is broken, and that's already a lot. Because as we know, there is only a minute distance from that broken window and all the rest. "Where is the egress?" asked Hakim Bey. It could be that it's right there, near that broken window and that pool of blood. It could also be that you will never see the word *exit* written anywhere ever again.

EPILOGUE

It's easier to run away from capitalism than to run away from one's family, of course. And that's why I've waited so long before talking about the latter. Newspapers enjoy putting names to faces, and so I might as well beat them to it. The late Antoine Riboud, long-time president of the BSN Group. He was my grandfather. His brothers. Jean, president of the Schlumberger Group. The other brother, Marc, the youngest. Photographer at Magnum, the one that I chose because he broke with the annoying fatality of current affairs.

I am the heir of a gigantic yogurt fortune. For a long time, I pretended it wasn't so. I wanted to protect myself from the heap of neuroses passed down through generations of my family. My grandfather was an *honorable* captain of industry. One factory then another. They said he leaned to the left. The refrigerator was full of his corporate acquisitions. The spring water everybody was buying. Evian. The beer everyone drank. Kronenbourg. The noodles everyone cooked. Panzani. Finally, the yogurt everyone was spooning into their mouths: Dannon. My grandfather often came to my parents' house a few miles outside of Paris for lunch. He never missed a chance to inspect the cupboards for signs of treason. When he found one of his competitors' brands . . . oh boy. A crisis. Into the trash can, boom, that would teach them. It was almost funny. The pure image of alienation. His brands were the story of his life, his pride and glory. And it's in this alienation that I lived, with the duty to consume the family's products, to buy family, to eat family, to shit family. In a very specific sense, my awareness of capitalism grew out of a gut feeling.

I especially remember the spring of 2001, the spring of the layoffs. Danone, Marks & Spencer, Moulinex, Bata. Family or humanity? Which side are you on? Progress or the inheritance? What do you pick? The law of returns or self-abasement, abasement of ourselves, of everyone who carried and kissed and fed us—which side? If we share blood, should I feel responsible? The only answer I have is: if one wants to avoid participating in the great slaughter, if you sincerely want to avoid reinforcing the captivity and the stranglehold, then you must desert, you must refuse power, you must drop out to avoid living the role that the machine wants you to live. You have to refuse to obey, you have to leave your position, fire yourself.

If I'm writing this book under a name other than the one I was given, it's not only to conceal myself. Not only to imagine that I am someone else, and forever place a distance between me and this pile of neuroses. It's not a mask. Merely an avatar that adds a little bit of something different into the sad destiny of the French elite. Camille, my first name, I chose on a winter night as I was leaving a small theater in Ivry-sur-Seine. It's the name of my great grandfather, doubtless a humanist, since he saved himself the agony of living through a second war by committing suicide in 1939. De Toledo is my father's other name, inherited from the Jews who were hounded out of Spain in 1492, at the dawn of the modern age. I like the way it sounds, for it evokes the aristocracy of exile. I hope that those who have understood me will call me Camille and will never again speak to me of grandfather, of gramps, of poppy, whatever, of that little piece of man who died yesterday or the day before yesterday. I have already forgotten. I kiss him one last time. And then I want to start all over.

Welcome to the land of the living, Camille de Toledo! It looks like a good time out there.

NOTES

1 Peter Sloterdijk, *Essai d'intoxication volontaire*, Paris, Calmann-Lévy, 1999, p. 9.

2 Jean-Paul Curnier, *Aggravation, 1989-1996*, Paris, Fourbis, 1997.

3 *France and Its Prisons*, presentation on the electronic bracelet before the French National Assembly by Eric Lallement, *documents d'information de l'Assemblée nationale*, 1997.

4 Albert Camus, *The Rebel*, Knopf, 1956, p.17

5 Francis Fukuyama, "The End of History?" *The National Interest*, #16, Summer, 1989, pp. 3-18.

6 ". . . A remarkable consensus concerning the legitimacy of liberal democracy as a system of government had emerged throughout the world over the past few years, as it conquered rival ideologies like hereditary monarchy, fascism, and most recently communism. More than that, however, I argued that liberal democracy may constitute the 'end point of mankind's ideological evolution' and the 'final form of human government,' and as such constituted the 'end of history.'" Francis Fukuyama, *The End of History and the Last Man*, Penguin, 1992. Also, see Gianni Vattimo, *La Fin de la modernité, nihilisme et hermeneutique dans la culture postmoderne*, Paris, Seuil, trad. Fr. Par Charles Alunni, 1987.

7 Arthur Danto, *Beyond the Brillo Box: The Visual Arts in Post-Historical Perspective*, Noonday Press/Farrar, Strauss, Giroux, New York, 1992, p. 9. The Belting text dates from 1983. As with Fukuyama's book, the title ends in a question mark: "Is the History of Art Over?" The title of Danto's book, published the following year, is more assertive and categorical, simply evoking "The End of Art."

8 The struggle between the *people of the end* and the *partisans of posts* is certainly not over yet. I would say only that there is a lag in the fighting. The new protest movement has produced a kind of cease-fire by shifting battlefields. Critical theory's deconstruction, for example, has been retired and replaced by direct action.

9 The French, as well as several other countries, chose to submit to a popular referendum the ratification of the Maastricht Treaty between the various members of the European Union who were adopting the new currency the Euro. It required that countries abide by certain macro-economic rules. Ironically, although that referendum succeeded, the French did decisively reject a proposed Constitution for the E.U., on May 29th, 2005, after publication of the French edition of this book.

10 Street name of Daniel Cohn-Bendit, a leader of the French student militants in 1968, now attached to the French Green Party and co-chairman of the Greens/Free European Alliance group in the European Parliament.

11 Serge July, leftist journalist and currently director of the left-leaning French daily *Libération*.

12 Bernard Henri-Lévy, former student leader during the 60s, now a major public intellectual.

13 Borrowed from the French punk magazine of the same name, published by the *Bazooka* group in the early 80s.

14 Isidor Isou (1928-?) Romanian artist and founder c. 1940 of the anti-Surrealist French literary movement "Lettrism," a precursor of Situationism.

15 See for example the work of the inspired puritans at *Adbusters*, a group of Canadian graphic designers who have taken advertising subversion to new heights.

16 See for example the book by Jean-Marie Dru, founder of the big French ad agency BDDP, *Disruption: Overturning Conventions and Shaking Up the Marketplace*, Jjohn Wiley & Sons, 1996.

[17] Two years later, in fall 1991, Debord makes Gallimard—the most prestigious French publishing house—his publisher. In 1992, *La Société du spectacle*, and *Commentaires sur la sociéte du spectacle* are reprinted with blank covers.

[18] "Who is everywhere? Who is aware? Who is powerful?" asked an IBM commercial in 1998. It claimed the three qualities of Goadhead for its own: Omnipresence, Omniscience and Omnipotence. Cited in *One Market Under God*, Thomas Frank, New York, Anchor Books, 2001.

[19] Eventually, the extension of the pension fund system will eliminate the existential possibility of criticizing capitalism. The fiscal obligation to withold for our retirement pensions will inexorably make shareholders of all of us, to the extent that exteriority to the system will become a thing of the past, eclipsed by a final interiority. What will the collective psychological consequences of such an existence be, this all-inclusive existence that so many seek to build? In such a situation, revolt will turn against the rebel. Violence against merchandise will become a kind of self-mutilation.

[20] Michel Foucault, *Discipline & Punish*.

[21] "La France face à ces prisons," *op cit.*, p. 263.

[22] Hakim Bey, *Immediatism*, (AK Press, 1994.)

[23] Naomi Klein, *No Logo*.

[24] Naomi Klein, *No Logo*.

[25] Naomi Klein, *No Logo*.

[26] Ignacio Ramonet, *Géopolitique du chaos*, Paris, Galilée, 1997, p. 49.

[27] Naomi Klein, *No Logo*.

[28] *The New Spirit of Capitalism*, Luc Boltanski and Ève Chiapello, Verso, 2005.

[29] Luc Boltanski and Ève Chiapello, *The New Spirit of Capitalism*.

[30] Luc Boltanski and Ève Chiapello, *The New Spirit of Capitalism*.

31 Naomi Klein, *No Logo*.

32 This is how I now understand the *symbolic* importance of the triple suicide of 1994: the Surrealist poet Ghérasim Luca in January, Kurt Cobain in April and Guy Debord in November. For me, they are beautiful rebel victims of the new captivity. Suddenly, they came to the conclusion that there was nothing left with which to confront reality.

33 Jean-Paul Curnier, *Manifeste*, Paris, Farrago-Léo Sheer, 2001, p. 8.

34 Subcommandante Marcos, *Ya Basta*, communique of the EZLN.

35 Gilles Châtelet, *Vivre et penser comme des porcs*, Paris, Exils, 1998; Paris, Gallimard, p. 89.

36 Manuel Castells, *La société en réseaux*, Paris, Fayard, 1998, ch. 6.

37 Here, I'm borrowing the distinction made by Boltanski and Chiapello in *The New Spirit of Capitalism*, Verso, 2005.

38 "Century" Foucault meant in the word's old-fashioned sense, the sense clerics meant when they used the French word "siè-cle," that is, the secular world and those who live in it.

39 Luc Boltanski and Ève Chiapello, *The New Spirit of Capitalism*.

40 Luc Boltanski and Ève Chiapello, *The New Spirit of Capitalism*.

41 Lucien Herr, the librarian of Paris's École Normale Supérieure, was one of the principal agents of the dissemination of Marx's texts in France at the end of the 19th century.

42 In his preface of 1946, Julien Benda places existentialist thought among the treasons. To make his case, he refers some remarks by Sartre cited by Thierry Maulnier in *L'Arche* in December 1945: "Since the writer has no way to escape, what we wish is that he fully embrace the times in which he lives— they are his only chance. They are made for him, and he for them. The indifference of Balzac faced with the insurrectional

days of 1848 is regrettable, the frightened incomprehension of Flaubert before the Commune is regrettable; and we regret them *in their name*. There was always something that they lacked. We do not want to overlook anything about our times. Maybe there are other eras that are more beautiful, but our era is ours. We have only this life to live, in the midst of *this* war, *this* revolution, perhaps." Paris, Grasset, coll. "Les cahiers rouges," 1975 reprint, p. 82.

43 Jean Genet, *The Thief's Journal*, Grove Press, 1964, p. 65.

44 Didier Eribon is quick to point out that there is a profound difference between Genet and Bataille. One is a voyeur of deviance, while the other is an actor. See Didier Eribon, *Une morale du minoritaire*, Paris, Fayard 2001.

45 Georges Bataille, *Story of the Eye*.

46 Gilles Deleuze and Félix Guattari, *The Anti-Œdipus*.

47 At this time Pan-Sonic was still called Panasonic. The pair was forced to change their name to avoid befing confused with the consumer electronics corporation.

48 See also David Rieder and Matthew Levy, *Enculturation*, vol. 3-1 Post-Digital Studies, Spring 2000, http://enculturation.gmu.edu.

49 Greil Marcus, *Lipstick Traces* , Harvard University Press 1990, p. 67.

50 William Gibson, *Neuromancer*.

51 William Gibson, *Neuromancer*.

52 William Gibson, *Neuromancer*.

53 Paul Ardenne in *L'image corps* suggests two other reasons behind the trend of "disappearancism": "[the aesthetic of the disappearance of the body] can also be explained by self-hatred and the guilt that racks the West. This principle of the unhappy conscience and dialectical fascination for the negative, this sacred love for self-degradation, this impenitent desire for castration . . . It is also the result of a situation of satiety—disgust over the surfeit of the figurative gift." Paul Ardenne, *L'image*

corps: *figure de l'humain dans l'art du XXe siècle*, Paris, Regard, 2001. p. 443-444.

54 William Gibson, *Neuromancer.*, op cit., p. 14.

55 Slogan of the digital artists' collective Etoy.

56 Gilles Deleuze and Félix Guattari, *Anti-Œdipus*. 1972. Trans. Robert Hurley, Mark Seem and Helen R. Lane. London: Althone, 1984. Vol. 1 of *Capitalism and Schizophrenia*, p. 35. 2 vols. 1972-1980. Trans. of *L'Anti-Œdipe*. Paris: Les Éditions de Minuit.

57 Gilles Deleuze and Félix Guattari, *Anti-Œdipus*.

58 Gilles Deleuze and Félix Guattari, *Anti-Œdipus*.

59 Gilles Deleuze and Félix Guattari, *Anti-Œdipus*.

60 Henry Miller, *Tropic of Cancer*.

61 "To the organ-machines, the body without organs opposes its smooth surface, opaque and stretched tight. To the interconnected flows, it opposes its amorphous, indifferent fluid." Gilles Deleuze and Félix Guattari, *Anti-Œdipus*.

62 "That will undoubtedly appear difficult to us to conceive, but half of the members of mankind never used a telephone in its life . . . Two civilizations are developing side by side, that of the privileged inhabitants of the electronic universe and that of the majorities for which the doors of the cyberspace hermetically remain closed . . . The reality is that 65% of the human population has never made a single telephone call and 40 % have no access to electricity. Manhattan has more telephone lines than in all the sub-Saharan Africa combined, " writes Jeremy Rifkin in *The Age of Access*.

63 Gilles Deleuze and Félix Guattari, *Anti-Œdipus*.

64 Jeremy Rifkin, *The Age of Access*.

65 Mallaury Nataf made her name through multiple appearances on a cult sitcom that ran during the end of the 90s in France, *Le Miel et les abeilles* ("Honey and the Bees"). She is also know for causing a scandal by appearing on a French talk show sans panties.

[66] Jeremy Rifkin, *The Age of Access.*

[67] Jeremy Rifkin, *The Age of Access.*

[68] Ed. "The Swing" (*Les hazards heureux de l'escarpolette*) (1767), a roccoco painting by French artist Jean-Honoré Fragonard, depicting an erotic scene where a slipper is about to fall from the foot of an aristocratic *coquette* as she is pushed on a swing.

[69] Gilles Châtelet, *Vivre et penser comme des porcs.*, *op. cit.*, p. 24.

[70] Kevin Kelly, *Out of Control, the Rise of the Neo-Biological Civilization*, Reading Addison-Wesley, Massachucetts, 1994. p. 20.

[71] Moore's Law was first formulated by the engineer Gordon Moore in 1964.

[72] Thomas Frank, *One Market Under God*, New York, Anchor Books, 2001.

[73] "Instead of Marx and his dialectic they have Moore's Law" writes Thomas Frank in *One Market Under God.*

[74] Julien Benda, *The Treason of the Intellectuals*, Benda is quoting Andrei Vychinsky, deputy Foreign Minister of the USSR.

[75] It's in forgetting this dimension of the body and in only addressing itself to the *skeeze* modernity that the European left lost the involuntary nomads, the formerly deeply-rooted members of the population. They did not see that their treason led millions of voters towards pure reaction and allowed dimension to become the monopoly of populists. That is the explanation for the sudden rise of the extreme right in Italy, Austria, France and even the Netherlands towards the end of the millenium.

[76] 1. Michel Le Bris, *D'or, de rêves et de sang, l'épopée de la filibuste, 1494-1588*, Paris, Hachette littératures, 2001, p. 12.

[77] *Le Monde*, 22-23 July, 2001.

[78] René Girard, *Deceit, Desire and the Novel: Self and Other in Literary Structure.*

[79] Hakim Bey is the pseudonym of Peter Lamborn Wilson.

80 Hakim Bey, *TAZ, The Temporary Autonomous Zone. Ontological Anarchy, Poetic Terrorism.* Autonomedia, 1991.

81 Hakim Bey, *TAZ, The Temporary Autonomous Zone.*

82 Hakim Bey, *Chaos: The Broadsheets of Ontological Anarchism.*

83 Hakim Bey, *TAZ, The Temporary Autonomous Zone.*

84 John Jordan, "The Art of Necessity: the Subversive Imagination of Anti-Road Protests and Reclaim the Streets." *The Cultural Resistance Reader.* Stephen Duncombe Ed. London: Verso, 2002 (p. 347-357)

85 ETA Hoffman, *Little Zachary.* My translation of a cited French translation (Michel Löwy and Robert Sayre, *Révolte et Mélancolie*, Paris, Payot, 1992.)

86 ETA Hoffman, *Little Zachary.*

87 Subcommandante Marcos, somewhere in the mountains of southeast Mexico, Chiapas, November 1985, letter to Eduardo Galeano, published in *Ya Basta!*

88 Friedrich Schlegel, *European Romanticism: Self Definition*, London, L. Furst, Methuen, 1980, p. 9.

89 Subcommandante Marcos, excerpt from "The Long March from Pain to Hope" ("La longue traversée de la douleur à l'espoir," Subcomandante Marcos, ¡*Ya Basta! Les insurgés zapatistes racontent un an de révolte au Chiapas*, Dagorno, París, 1994.)

90 http://www.abcnorio.org. The squat is located in New York at Rivington Street and Clinton Avenue, in the East Village.

91 Steven Wray, "The Electronic Disturbance Theater and Electronic Civil Disobedience," 1998, Ch. 2 complet ref. http://transcriptions.english.ucsb.edu/archive/courses/liu/englis h236/materials/class20notes.html

92 Pikka Himanen, *The Hacker Ethic and the Spirit of the Information Age*, New York, Random House, 2001.

93 This is why it is so dangerous that States and their police interrupt the semantic game by using force. When they do, they exit the symbolic. In Genoa, when the carabiniers charges and fired

real bullets, they violated the *rules of the game* that had sought to est the scene for a *semantic* confrontation.

94 Marcos, interview with *La Tribune de Genève*, April 21, 1995.

95 In the first half of the 90s, the streets were the new incarnation's privileged stage: towards 1993, Reclaim the Streets in England and the first Argentine piqueteros put the occupation of the street at the center of their strategies. "In this network [i.e. that of the information society]," wrote sociologist Manuel Castells in *The Rise of the Network Society*, "no location exists on its own, since situations are are defined by flux. Moreover, the communication network is the fundamental spatial configuration: sites do not disappear, but their logic and their meaning is determined by the network." In the shadow of this absorbtion, the streets were simultaneously the allies of capital and their enemies. As transit spaces for material goods, they were thus also the territory of the services and the information directing the commodity flows. But they are also sites of resistance to the extent that they constitute a trace of distances that must be crossed, of trajectories. Embedded within them is the awareness of matter, dimension, length and longing—and eventually, the march of spaces across time. It is on and through the street that the *piqueteros* of Argentina and the activists of Reclaim the Streets made one feel how matter resists the flux of financial liquidities. By blocking it, they reintroduced the flux to the dimension of bodies.

96 George McKay, *Senseless Acts of Beauty, Cultures of Resistance Since the Sixties*, Verso, 1996.

97 Michael Löwy and Robert Sayre, *Révolte et Mélancolie.*, *op. cit.*, p. 22-23.

98 Hakim Bey, TAZ, *The Temporary Autonomous Zone*.

99 Robert Musil, *The Man Without Qualities*.